# MORE *than* Welcome

# MORE *than* Welcome

*Learning to Embrace Gay, Lesbian,
Bisexual, and Transgendered
Persons in the Church*

## Maurine C. Waun

**Chalice Press**
St. Louis, Missouri

Cover: Samuel H. Domínguez
Interior design: Elizabeth Wright

This book is printed on acid-free, recycled paper.

Visit Chalice Press on the World Wide Web at
www.chalicepress.com

9  8  7  6  5  4  3  2          00  01  02  03 04

**Library of Congress Cataloging–in–Publication Data**

Waun, Maurine C.
   More than welcome : learning to embrace gay, lesbian, bisexual, and transgendered persons in the church / by Maurine C. Waun
       p.    cm.
   ISBN 0-8272-2325-0
   1. Homosexuality–Religious aspects–Christianity. 2. Christian gays. I. Title.
BR115.H6W38  1999
261.8'35766–dc21                                              98–43562
                                                                CIP

Printed in the United States of America

To my precious grandchildren,
in hopes that the Church of THEIR grandchildren
might be fully embracing of all people

# Table of Contents

# Acknowledgments

My fondest appreciation goes to a group of people who encouraged me as I worked on this project. First and foremost Bruce Dobler, whose kind words, critiques, and enthusiasm helped me all along the way. Other persons who offered valuable comments and insight are Carenda Baker, William Doebler, Joel Garrett, Butch Hilliard, Heidi Jasiewicz, the late Willie Ludlow, David Morse, Sara Penn-Strah, and a Franciscan monk who dare not be named, as well as computer consultant LeAndra Speaks and personal cheerleaders Marion Bannister and Norman Otto.

I am grateful to my colleagues Peter D. Weaver and David F. Keller who offered their moral support, and to certain members of the congregation of the First United Methodist Church of Pittsburgh who have been following this project with positive interest.

Of course, the stories themselves emerged from the lives of countless persons who have shared their lives with me, and who can claim credit for imparting greater compassion and understanding of their truth.

Special thanks go to Jon L. Berquist, my editor, for shepherding this book through a long and winding journey.

# Preface

This book is for you if you are a person of faith who is wrestling with the issue of homosexuality, especially concerning the place of gay and lesbian persons in the life of the church. Perhaps you care about social injustice and prejudice against a substantial percentage of our society. You probably do not like the hate and exclusion preached by the radical right, nor do you necessarily want the topic of sexual variance openly discussed. My purpose here is not to refute the scriptural arguments claiming that homosexuality is a sin; many other books do that, and you can find the scripture citations and the titles of many helpful books listed in the Appendix. I have already read enough books, talked to enough gay, lesbian, bisexual, and transgendered persons, and thought about the issue enough to know this: neither homosexual orientation nor homosexual behavior is a sin. Moreover, we cannot continue to debate and batter each other with scriptural proofs and counter-proofs until we are even more polarized about the compatibility of homosexuality with Christian teaching. If the church keeps arguing, it will be so far beyond the misery of gay, lesbian, bisexual, and transgendered persons that we will have lost most of these sisters and brothers for good.

This book is an experiential approach to the question of the church and sexual orientation because that is where my pastoral work has most connected with personal pain in the world of so many persons who seek counsel. We cannot use scriptural arguments to make conclusive statements because they are too ambiguous. There is really no clear way of interpreting the seven passages that are most often referred to when discussing homosexuality. Other ways of identifying Christian core truths include reason and tradition, neither of which gives us any more clarity here than does scripture, because reason and tradition are tied to interpretations of scriptures. As two people examine the same passages, what is reasonable to one person is unacceptable to another. A particular belief system is adopted and then passed down by the general church community from generation to generation as Christian tradition, until the time when a new experiential truth emerges from the culture to challenge and change that tradition. This process has been visible over centuries in the church with the liberation of slaves, women, people of color, and other oppressed groups.

Gay, lesbian, bisexual, and transgendered persons are no longer able to integrate in their lives Christian tradition, which condemns non-heterosexual behavior, because the truth of their own experience has proved more reasonable and compatible with scriptures that proclaim love, inclusion, and the beauty of God's creation in all its variety. The pain of sexual minorities is, at this moment, so ponderous and so enormous that the church is missing the mark by not even daring to look beyond the scriptural debate toward the hurts and issues of persons who are bravely and genuinely struggling in their everyday experience.

Meanwhile, many millions of beautiful and gifted people often feel terribly alone because the church has not yet noticed the depth and breadth of their ongoing pain in our neighborhoods, families, and work places—wondering how to talk about it, where to go for spiritual guidance, and what do to with a moral code that has precious little to do with the circumstances of living embodied life and being in a relationship as a gay, lesbian, bisexual, or transgendered person.

Where is the church, the mainstream church, for gay, lesbian, bisexual, and transgendered persons? It is nowhere. We have rejected sexual minorities as sinners or as people who must be healed of an illness. (I will elaborate on the illness model in Chapter 12.) Sexual orientation, whether homosexual, heterosexual or something in between, is simply the way a person is created—part of the wondrous variety of the natural order. The mainstream church has fallen way behind knowledge already accepted in the human sciences about sexual variance, and in doing so we have made ourselves the irrelevant enemy. Wake up, church! We are way behind on this issue and we are losing ground fast. We talk about finding new avenues for evangelism—well, here is one. The church has an opportunity to be inclusive beyond anything we could ever imagine. So far, the church has failed miserably to attract gay, lesbian, bisexual, and transgendered persons because it is too busy preaching condemnation. *Of course* they are staying away! And it's our own fault. All sexual orientations need the church, yes. But the church's need for each orientation is even greater—to teach us, to gift us with special insights, to walk with us as we learn about life-giving relationships together.

Read my story. Read the stories of a few persons whom I have had the privilege of knowing in my ministry, while they have patiently appreciated my willingness to learn from them. I hope you will learn from these stories as well, and in the process plant your flag in a place that will open church doors and hearts. Hence, the alienation from the sexual minority community will end, and we will truly be the church that Jesus Christ meant us to be: one of love, compassion, and service, and one where we lay down our lives for one another.

# PART I

# Forming
# the
# Question

# CHAPTER 1

# Beginning in Darkness

*"I felt like a child playing with pebbles on the shore when the ocean of truth lay all about me."* —Isaac Newton

How could I have grown up totally ignorant of the very issue that, in my adulthood, would command so much of my attention and then become the focus of the most meaningful ministry of my career? What was it about my early experience and development that kept me in a place of naivete and darkness about this until, through a very long and confusing process, I arrived at a way of thinking that I never could have predicted in myself?

The issue is homosexuality. It wasn't part of my early awareness; it wasn't a word that anyone used around me; it wasn't part of my social upbringing in any way. As I became more aware of homosexuality in the larger world, the very idea of it clashed with my accepted map of reality. As I tried to incorporate the idea into my belief system, I found that I had no internal point of reference with which to understand it.

As my map of reality became larger and was redefined by new surroundings, I turned to trusted teachers, mentors, and institutions to help me sort out my ignorance and confusion.

Because those teachers, mentors and institutions addressed the issue in such a way that there were still big gaps left between their explanations and my emerging experience of reality, I began to doubt the truth of what they had to say. My inner voice was saying "Uh-oh. Something is wrong. Something doesn't add up. Someone isn't telling me everything. How can I rely on truths that don't seem to address the pain and oppression that I see around me?"

I find it troubling when the truth I have most come to doubt is that which comes from the church. Certainly that is the very place where we hope to find time-honored truths that can withstand healthy doubting and questioning. It is not easy to know which way to move—yet move we must, when we find ourselves in deep conflict with traditional church teaching. Do we question our own motives, our own perceptions, our own map of reality? Of course we do. But having questioned and tested our own position in relation to church teaching, we must be willing to live honestly and without fear of the church. We move on in this process, to a place that is more relevant to our experience and understanding. We must have the courage to follow Christ instead of the church. Revelation happens only at that moment when experience, tradition and belief seem to come together into an "Aha" that satisfies until the next disparity occurs.

Homosexuality is, for me, the issue that has most profoundly challenged the congruity between the beliefs handed down to me by the church and my own map of reality. The lack of information, teaching or discussion on this topic throughout my childhood left me completely unprepared when, as an ordained clergy person whose denomination's official position is that the practice of homosexuality is incompatible with Christian teaching, (*Methodist Book of Discipline*, 1996), I found myself in pastoral situations where tradition clashed painfully and dramatically with what was given to me as established doctrine and with the rationale upon which it is based.

At this moment in my career (after seventeen years in the pastorate) I stand in direct opposition to most Christians' views on the practice of homosexuality. While the mainstream church says that the practice of homosexuality is incompatible with Christ's teaching, I disagree. I believe that homosexual practices are compatible with Christian teaching. I believe that the rationale the church has used for centuries to condemn homosexuality and its practice is faulty and distorted. How did I come to this place? What happened along the journey of my life and spirit to cause me to now hold this "unorthodox" belief? Somewhere, somehow along the way I felt a certain nagging "Uh-oh"—a dissonance between what the church was teaching and what I was experiencing that threw me into a quandary of doubt and questioning that finally settled into the "Aha" of a new approach. What was it? How do I describe this transformation in such a way that it might challenge the thinking of others within the church so that together we can seek the appropriate place and role of the church in this matter?

In order for you to understand what a tremendous shift this present belief about homosexuality represents for me, I need to trace its evolution. This includes a brief history of what has shaped me along the way. I must begin in the place where I grew up—in Romeo, Michigan—the heartland of America, where differences were noticed and feared. Sameness was valued and rewarded.

Growing up in the tiny town of Romeo in the fifties and early sixties was a bit like being in a 3-D Norman Rockwell painting. It was a very different kind of world than the one I live in now. This picturesque little town was more removed, more protected, more relaxed and certainly more traditional than the sprawling city of Detroit barely thirty miles to the south. The tree-lined streets defined quiet neighborhoods of mostly Victorian homes, and on the fringes were newer ranch-type houses, which were built in subdivisions that were just beginning to overtake the peach and apple orchards that surrounded the area. In those days my brother and I played softball and caught frogs down by the creek during the summer, and we did our homework, built models, and skated on the frozen lakes and ponds in the winter.

School was the centerpiece of my social life. I played with the same boys and girls who were in my class and they were always invited to my birthday parties. In those days the school system was small enough that I started kindergarten with a group of children that stayed together until we all graduated from high school. Occasionally a new kid would arrive and would be

thought of as "the new kid" for many years later, especially if
that boy or girl was from the city—they were always set apart
somehow by not having the common bond and background
that the rest of us had. There were a few African American
students scattered throughout the grades, all of them children of
families that lived on the other side of the tracks.

There was a Catholic church at the edge of town that had its
own elementary school. When those kids were finally assimi-
lated into the public school in the ninth grade they usually re-
tained a "they" identity until graduation from high school.

That is how we handled diversity back then. Differences
were not appreciated nor discussed much if at all; certainly they
were not celebrated unless in the most extraordinary circumstances. Playgrounds and social activities were segregated along
traditional gender lines. I suppose this was the very place where
gender stereotypes were most lived and learned.

It was hard for me to understand why one or two of the girls
would subject themselves day after day to the torments of cross-
gendered play when it seemed so much easier to just play with
the other girls. Eventually, however, they became true jocks who
weren't fully accepted by the girls or found attractive for relationships by the boys—especially since those girls seemed to go
out of their way to deny their femininity, according to the traditions and stereotypes we were assimilating. In addition, although
we rarely talked about it, we girls thought these misfits were at
best weird and at worst foolish; as time went on we had less and
less in common with them and so did not include them. The
thought that some of my friends might have had a different
sexual orientation never entered my mind. How could it? No
one ever gave me information one way or the other about it. I
never knew it existed. I now wonder how the sexual minorities
among us ever survived their adolescence.

My map of reality was woefully small in that picture-perfect
rural town in midwest America. When I went away to Michigan
State University my worldview expanded so fast that I was in
culture shock for about a year. I lived in a large women's dormi-
tory where there were girls from everywhere—small towns, big
cities, other states, other countries and cultures, and other races.
I learned about makeup and hair teasing and smoking cigarettes.

I went to off-campus parties and found out about drinking and sex. For the first time in my life I was trying to maintain my balance between responsibility and experimentation, personal integrity and adventure, goals and freedom. It was a wonderful, awful time. The differences that were so avoided, overlooked, and unappreciated in my upbringing were unavoidable and blatantly present every day on campus, and learning to cope with them was both exhilarating and terrifying. Traditions and stereotypes were being shattered left and right, yet the subject of homosexuality was still not addressed or even raised.

As a sophomore I enrolled in a study-abroad program in which I traveled to Switzerland and lived for a year with a Swiss family. What an adventure for a naive nineteen-year-old girl from small town America! There were lots of men who were very attentive to me but that was more frightening than flattering at the time. One of my holiday trips took me to Spain where, having met a local Spaniard who persuaded me to go out alone with him, I found myself cornered in the back room of a restaurant being urged to take off my clothes. As I struggled to resist and push the man away he jeered at me, saying that the reason I didn't want to make love with him was because I was a "lesbian." Now because of his Spanish accent I didn't understand what he had said, and so he repeated it again and again. I honestly did not know what the word meant or even if the word was Spanish or English. I had never heard it before but I figured that it described someone who was abnormal in some way. I was confused, frightened, and humiliated. All I could do was cry as I broke free and ran away. Only much later did I have an occasion to look up the word "lesbian" and find out what it meant.

Years went by. I finished college, married, and had two babies. Again there was no inkling that sexual minorities shared my world, but occasionally I would hear a gay joke. I would laugh and then forget about the subject that prompted it, as it was always accompanied by a nervous sense of discomfort.

At mid-life I left my teaching job and became a student at Pittsburgh Theological Seminary. The next time I encountered the topic of homosexuality was in a more formal way in an ethics class. That was really the first opportunity I had ever had to reflect on this subject in any way, but more especially in the context of Christian teaching. I had been given an assignment to choose an issue from a posted list of subjects, examine relevant scriptures, and then develop an ethical argument based on those scriptures in favor of or against the chosen issue. I selected homosexuality. I don't know why. Perhaps it was because I had had so little exposure to the topic and I wanted to explore it. Maybe I opted for it because it seemed like such an easy task: to find scriptures to condemn homosexuality.

The scripture I chose was one of the Creation sections of Genesis (Genesis 2:18–25). Perhaps I did this because of a joke that I had heard about God creating Adam and Eve, not Adam and Steve. I quickly discovered a couple of things. First, I really didn't have enough time and expertise to do adequate exegetical work on this passage. Second, I became easily confused while forming my argument, in light of some of the ethical strategies we had studied. I knew I wanted to argue against homosexuality, but I couldn't find a substantial reason to do so in the book of Genesis, and it was too late to begin again with a different set of scriptures. The paper was due in two days. When I came right down to my persuasive conclusion, I finally settled for a "natural law" argument. Homosexuality, I posed, was not natural, and so it was unethical, wrong, sinful. My professor had a field day with that one. His criticisms were among the most instructive lessons I received while in seminary. I had been sure that he would disapprove of homosexuality; after all, wasn't he a seminary professor and an ordained clergyman? And didn't everybody know that homosexuality was wrong? It certainly wouldn't take much of an argument to prove that. Yet I had failed to do so. He also pointed out that by using the natural law stance I could prove that wearing clothes, shaving my legs, growing flowers indoors, and dyeing cloth were equally sinful. In addition, he went on to show how one could use the same text to argue in favor of homosexuality.

After suffering such an attack on my logic and realizing that it is possible for intelligent Christian people to arrive at differing conclusions based on the same supposedly firm ethical grounds, I was shaken. It was definitely another stretch on my map of reality, as it now had to include the fact that all Christians do *not* agree that homosexuality is sinful.

Later in my seminary years, I took a class in rhetorical strategy where we were asked to sign up for a debate assignment on various topics. When I saw the list, there were three topics remaining, one of which was to debate for or against the ordination of homosexual candidates for ministry. For whatever reasons, this seemed to be the most appealing subject to me. Possibly I wanted to redeem my earlier fiasco in the ethics class by doing a better job on this assignment, and so I made the decision to do it. At any rate, there were two spaces by each debate, one to sign up "For" and the other "Against." At that same moment, another student said that he wanted to debate this topic also. I asked him why, and he answered, "Arguing against the ordination of homosexuals is a piece of cake. All I'll need is my church's official policy and the Bible and I'll win hands down!" With a flourish, he signed his name in the "Against" column. Then he laughed and disappeared.

Now, there was something about the attitude of my colleague that really offended me. I thought, "You sanctimonious, arrogant son of a gun, it *couldn't* be that easy. I'll show you!" And so I signed up to defend the ordination of homosexuals, determined to outdo my opponent as an exercise in rhetorical strategy. After all, wasn't that what I was to learn from the class?

My next step was to take enough time to do adequate research from scripture and other sources so that I wouldn't fall into the same time crunch that had thwarted my efforts before. I mentioned my task to another student who suggested that I interview a friend of his named John who was doing doctoral work at the seminary, someone who would know the theological arguments from having done lengthy study in the area of homosexuality. He also told me that John was gay and an ordained minister, and that he would probably welcome the opportunity to share his journey and knowledge with me for purposes of my assignment, because he had suffered some abuses at the hands of the church.

All at once, the feelings I had associated with my limited experience of homosexuality (the humiliation of my episode in Spain, the discomfort around "gay" jokes, the inadequacy of my argument in that first ethics paper, the confusion of differences of opinion) all surfaced and converged in that moment when I realized that I would be knowingly meeting and talking with a homosexual person for the first time in my life.

I was uneasy. In spite of my ignorance in this area, I admit that I had formed some stereotypes based on the few jokes and comments I had heard throughout my life. I wondered if this man would behave appropriately. Part of me thought it was disgusting that he would admit that he was gay, while at the same time I was grateful that he was there to help me. The only problem was finding the courage to call him to ask for an appointment to talk with him. Somehow I managed to do that and even stammered out a "Thank you" as we set the time for me to go to his apartment.

At the agreed time I arrived at his door and rang the bell. I was very tense. My lunch sat like a rock in my stomach. I really didn't know what to expect. I thought that perhaps John would be deformed or weird or be dressed like a woman. What if someone saw me going into his apartment? Would I be safe in there? Would he say something that would embarrass me or make me want to run for my life? I could feel the discomfort mounting as I waited for John to answer the door.

Finally the door opened. There before me stood a very handsome man with sparkling blue eyes, beautiful brown wavy hair, and a moustache. John was tall and slim and was the kind of man who really looked good in stylish clothes. If I hadn't been so scared, his quick smile might have put me at ease, but I guess I wasn't prepared for the friendliness that I encountered. He greeted me warmly and invited me in.

When I stepped into his living room my eyes darted restlessly here and there looking for clues that John was gay. I thought there might be an erotic painting on the wall, or a bawdy magazine on the coffee table, or some other suggestion of repulsive bodily activity that I didn't care to think about. I saw the doorway to John's bedroom and my eyes quickly turned away in embarrassment as I sat down on the couch. The apartment was decorated in a distinctive manner, consistent with John's taste in clothes and the light jazz music that played from the stereo in the background. He offered me something to drink. "No thanks," I said. I wanted to make this visit short and to the point.

I took a spiral notebook from my book bag and flipped open the cover to begin writing. I explained in more detail what my assignment was for the debate and asked him to give me anything that he thought might help. John began by reviewing the scriptures associated with homosexuality itself. Because of his theological expertise he was able to interpret each passage in a way that challenged the conventional views. He cited resources and authors for further reference (see the Appendix). I wrote furiously, since I had not heard anything like this before, and I wanted to record every point he made that might help me to win my debate. For the seven scripture passages that are commonly used to condemn homosexuality, John used his exegetical skill and knowledge of the ancient languages to disprove every standard argument.

After going over the scriptures, John began to explain how I might formulate arguments based on Christ's mandate to love and include, in relationship to the church and its mission in the world today. By then I was fascinated by his perspective and profoundly impressed by his knowledge and command of the original languages of the scriptures. He was extremely articulate and spoke clearly with a strong sense of authority on this topic. I could see that this meeting was going to be neither short nor to the point. I accepted his offer for something to drink as we entered a third area of discussion—his experience as an ordained minister with the church.

John had been a rising star in his denomination. His seminary record when he received his Master of Divinity degree was impeccable. After graduation he had been called to pastor a mid-sized church in a busy suburb. There he worked hard to build up the programs, increase the membership and giving, and to help the church to reach out with Christ's love into the community as they found more and more hands-on ministry opportunities. After a few years of extraordinary personal and professional success, someone in the regional church hierarchy found out that John was gay.

What happened next was a series of events that can only be described as an ecclesiastical nightmare. John was brought before the governing denominational body, where he was publicly questioned about his orientation. He didn't disclose to me whether he admitted that he was gay or if he lied and they found out about it some other way. It seemed to me, as I listened, that it probably wouldn't have mattered in any case, as the outcome was that the judicatory officials stripped John of his ordination and removed him immediately from the church.

The people he served were devastated. They had worked with John, their pastor, for years. They knew him to be devoted and wonderfully well-suited to their congregation. Some of the people wrote letters to the executives who were responsible for the decision, others protested in other ways. A few even thought that the congregation should break away from the denomination, start their own church and receive John back as their pastor of choice. There was a small number who were shocked to know that John was gay and did not agree with the efforts to advocate for him, but for the most part the issue for this church was not John's sexual orientation. Rather, it was the unjust way that both he and the congregation had been treated in the matter, with no regard for the relationship that they had built or the ministry that they had established under John's leadership. In the end, everyone lost. John was forced out of the ordained ministry and the church people were robbed of their beloved pastor against their objections, all because the national denominational policy stated that the ordination of homosexuals was not acceptable. As I listened to the deep pain that John suffered over this tragedy in his life, I found that the feelings of anxiety I had when I entered John's apartment were replaced by a growing anger in the core of my being toward a system that could condemn, oppress, and carry out acts of tremendous injustice in the name of religion. The fact that the system in question was the institutional church made it all that much more deplorable. What about John's gifts and call to ministry? What about his superior leadership skills? What about the results of ministry that John and the church had achieved? How could any of that possibly be affected by a person's sexual orientation? What conceivable difference would it make? I was appalled.

But John's problems had begun long before this. Even the church-related seminary was not a safe haven for John. Shortly after his arrival in the student housing apartments, he suffered abuse. Some of the people at the seminary, sensing he was gay, insisted that he be thrown out or that, at the very least, he be forced to live off campus, instead of in a seminary-owned apartment. One afternoon, after a long and tiring day of classes and lectures, John walked home to find that someone had scraped the word "faggot" across the side of his new car with an ice pick. Yet John told me all of this with such calm and grace. He had lived through this horrible pain, had wrestled with what it meant, and was hoping to redeem it somehow by trying to bring something good out of it. He was a scholar and a theologian, and he would make his contribution to the church by teaching at the seminary level. The wounds caused by the violence done to him by other Christians were healing even as he told me his story; even as, in the telling, his words caused new wounds in me. It is the pain and injustice of John, and many others whose stories I would hear, that would eventually grow and culminate in a transformation and passion in my own life around the issue of homosexuality.

After two hours with John and many pages of notes, I got up to leave and begin working on my debate arguments. As I passed by John's bedroom door, my eyes did quickly scan the room. The most prominent feature of decor that I saw there was a simple wooden cross hanging over John's bed. It was at that moment I had to ask God to forgive me for allowing my initial fears to run away with my sense of genuine acceptance and caring for this new friend. I had survived my first known encounter with a homosexual person, and I knew that I would try not to permit such fear to stand between me and another human being ever again. This experience was truly shocking, fundamental, and formative in my journey of ministry.

The day of the debate arrived, and I was fully prepared. My colleague breezed into class as promised, with denominational and biblical references cited as arguments. We debated for thirty minutes. I won. Not only that, I won big—for me, for John, for anyone in the audience with a passion for justice and the gospel, for Christ, and for those persons who, in quiet desperation, watch and wait for a word of grace from the church as they struggle with their own sexual orientation.

# CHAPTER 2

# My Son Larry

*"That religion cannot be right, that a person is the worse for having." —William Penn*

All of my prior experiences were formative, but most valuable were the lessons I learned as I entered my first position as an ordained pastor. The church where I came to serve as part of the pastoral staff was First United Methodist Church of Pittsburgh—a flagship church in a location that was at the hub of several neighborhoods, each with a different set of issues. In one direction there were the university and medical communities. In another, high rise apartments. In still another, families of all types. There were business districts and further down the boulevard, urban blight. It was possible to look out windows from the different sides of the church building and find a different type of ministry in each direction. The neighborhood was scattered with persons of varying economic, educational, and ethnic backgrounds. There were homeless persons, addicts of all types, yuppies, elderly, average homeowners, and Section 8 tenants who lived in subsidized housing. Some of the persons who attended the church were long-time members and some were second-generation people who drove in from the suburbs.

15

Many students, medical personnel, and young adult professionals came, along with neighborhood families, older couples, and singles of all ages. Although largely white, the congregation was composed of various races, including Asian Americans and people from foreign countries such as Burma, Jamaica, and Zimbabwe.

Almost diagonally across from the church was Shadyside Hospital, where our staff would occasionally get called to pray with someone whom we did not know. It became apparent, in the mid- to late eighties, that we were beginning to be called to visit HIV positive patients, although no one ever said so directly.

By 1987 it seemed to us that, by virtue of our location, it would be appropriate to offer a community-wide educational seminar about AIDS. Our target audience would include persons from the church community, the educational community, and certain service providers—those who most needed information and reassurance, we thought. After months of planning, and with the seminar about three weeks away, we identified our church building as the location of the seminar by putting up a large sign on the lawn. It said simply "AIDS Seminar," the date, and the church office phone number.

Just a few days before the event I received a phone call that would change the shape of my life and ministry, as well as that of my congregation, forever. The call was from a fellow named Larry. It happened that he had just been discharged from nearby Shadyside Hospital and saw the "AIDS Seminar" sign in the churchyard as he was on his way home. He carefully copied down the phone number because he wanted to find out exactly what we were up to. Larry couldn't imagine how a church could have anything to do with something like AIDS and asked for specific information about who would be making presentations and so on.

After talking with me at length, Larry then confessed that he himself had AIDS, and this was the reason why he had such an interest in what we were doing. He had grown to distrust the church, but because he had liked everything I said about the upcoming seminar, he offered to help with one of the presentations. I reacted to this suggestion about the same way I did when I knew I was going to meet John. I was scared. I mustered a weak "Thank you" and kept telling myself that the participants who would gather in my church on the day of the seminar would be perfectly safe...perfectly safe...perfectly safe. Of course, I knew this in my head, but my guts were wrenching with irrational fears, yet I knew that letting Larry come and help with one of the presentations was the right thing to do. I accepted his offer, and I knew that I would deal with whatever consequences my decision would present, at a later time. I sent Larry the same letter of confirmation that all other presenters received, along with a name tag to wear as he entered the building, so that I would know who he was and be able to greet him properly, since we had not yet met.

The day of the seminar arrived. I had stationed myself near the main entrance. All at once there stood before me a rather thin, tall man with reddish brown hair, a beard, and a moustache, looking somewhat nervous. He was wearing a name tag that said "Larry." This was the moment of truth for me. I had learned from my experience with John that I would never let my fear stand between me and another person, yet I was very much aware of my fear of AIDS and this real live person who was suffering from it. I knew that I had to greet this man as genuinely as I would greet any other person that day, because that was what I believed Jesus would have wanted me to do; in my heart I wanted to do it. I was extremely self-conscious and probably stammered a bit. I felt that old rock in my stomach again, but I reached out anyway. I succeeded in welcoming Larry graciously and escorting him to the room where he would speak, all the while babbling distractedly as we made our way through the hallways. Larry, meanwhile, warmed up quickly to me, flashing me his winsome smile and disarming wit, and I found myself feeling a bit more relaxed, even as I was relieved finally to drop him off at the assigned room.

When I decided to return later to hear Larry's presentation, every seat was filled and several people were standing along the wall. My timing was perfect. I entered from the back of the audience at just the moment when the main speaker was introducing Larry. Applause brought him to the front of the group, where he began to speak in a mild yet confident southern drawl. He started by saying that he had been born and raised in Texas, where his parents had taken him to a neighborhood church throughout his childhood. Over the years they had survived their ups and downs as a family but his folks were very strict and held conservative Christian values. As Larry grew into adulthood they measured him more and more against their own predetermined expectations for his life and seemed to be more and more disappointed all the time. This was especially true now.

Larry recounted the darkest day of his life, which occurred two years previously, after having learned of his AIDS diagnosis. At the time, he was out of work and decided to approach his parents to see if they might take him in during the awful transition time without financial stability and insurance coverage. He remembered saying, "Mom, Dad, I have good news and I have bad news. The good news is that I am gay. The bad news is that I have AIDS." That was apparently as much as Larry had to say. His parents were horrified. They became violently angry. Monstrous name-calling ensued. Larry was labeled "queer," "no-good bastard," "sinner," and worse. He was told to "Go to hell, faggot, and never come back. The devil's gonna burn you good!" They then kicked him out of their home and said they never wanted to see or hear from him again. He was to never again refer to himself as their son or to them as his parents. He should go away and die so they could be rid of him forever.

As I sat and listened to Larry's story I couldn't help but hear the deep woundedness that was present in his voice as he told what had happened to him. He went on to relate how, because of a few contacts he had made, he decided to move to Pittsburgh to find service agencies that could help him in this horrible time. So, here he was, trying to start over, to build a life in a new place, surrounded by strangers, doing his best to get by and take care of himself.

I thought about Larry's pain. The part of my heart that is a mother felt as if it had been stabbed with a knife. Suddenly I knew that I would take this man's side, even if my whole ministry depended upon it. I realized that a child's worst fear is that someday "Mother" might go away, and for this grown "child" the nightmare had come true. For what reason? Because he was gay? Because he had AIDS? Was this a reason for a mother to say to her own child, "Go to hell and never try to contact me again"? How could anyone be so cruel and so condemning to her own flesh and blood, especially because of religious values? I knew in my heart of hearts that Jesus would be deeply grieved by such a blatant misinterpretation of his teaching. I was filled with compassion for Larry, while at the same time I admired his courage for standing tall in front of this group to tell his story for the sole purpose of helping others to understand. He was so articulate and persuasive, affable and talented. I knew that I would be one that would try to help heal the tremendous torment in Larry's heart.

Within two days of the seminar I wrote Larry a note and sent it to his home. I told him how his story had affected me and that perhaps I could act as his mother. I said that I didn't know what this would mean to him, but that I was willing to do whatever it took; I would bake cookies, take him to lunch, whatever mothers do. What did he think? How did he feel about such a strange invitation? Soon I heard from Larry. He was deeply moved by my note. In fact, he told me later that he cried for several hours after reading it. He didn't want to answer me right away because he had a lot of feelings about the "church," and my being a pastor might present difficulties for him. He wanted to come and meet with me to talk things out and then he would decide what to do about my offer.

I remember the day Larry came into my office. He sat in the brown leather chair in front of the stained glass windows so that the filtered light framed his face as we talked. Larry's hair was wavy and full and his hazel eyes were filled with searching. Even though he was much too thin he was a very handsome man with a distinctive style that was apparent in his clothes, jewelry, and designer glasses. He was delightfully humorous and candid and confessed to me that he was amazed that, when he had come in and out of the church on the day of the seminar, lightning had not struck him dead! He had been carefully taught as a child that gays go to hell to burn for all eternity. Yet here he was, in a church; moreover, in the associate pastor's office, and he was still alive!

We talked for about four hours. Larry told me about his young adulthood and how, because of cultural and family expectations, he had married, fathered two boys, and then struggled for years with his sexual identity. He knew during those years that he was miserably unhappy, but he didn't really know why until it happened: one day he fell hopelessly in love—with a man. He was so totally shaken and confused by this that he was thrown into denial. After all, gays were terrible sinners, were they not? Yet denial could only postpone the inevitable—Larry finally went through a painful divorce and ended up following his heart into a same-sex relationship, where, for the first time in his life, he felt a sense of personal integrity and confidence in who he was.

I realized that Larry did not choose to be gay. He would not willfully choose to be part of such a stigmatized minority. He simply discovered that he was gay and that he was created so by God. At that point in his life, Larry allowed himself to accept the reality of the givens he was born with and to move forward with his existence.

I listened while Larry went into all the shadows of his life. It was as if he needed to bare his soul before the one person who could represent for him both his mother and his church, to see if I would still find him valued and loveable—to see if I would go back on my instinct to want to include him in my circle of love. What I heard was the earnest yearning of a spirit trying to find its way back to God, the God who had created Larry and who loved him unconditionally. He needed desperately to be reassured of this love so that true healing could begin, not only spiritual healing but physical as well.

At the end of that first time together, Larry and I cried tears of—I don't know—relief, peace, shared hurt. I prayed with him for comfort and healing for all the unjust and cruel things that had happened to him, and also gratitude for his good fortune in finding a way back to God. After all this, Larry pulled me into his arms and hugged me with warm, genuine affection and called me "Mama." I now had something I had never had before—a son.

Now it was time to introduce him to my daughters at home and to the church. How would I explain this? I was especially concerned that parishioners might see my "adoption" of Larry as rescuing him, as overstepping my pastoral authority. I had never done this type of thing before and it felt very risky. Yet, I thought, what is the love of God if it cannot break through at a time like this for a healing that touches more than just the spirit?

I tackled the home front first, where my daughters and I lived together. My first challenge was to bring Larry home to meet the girls. What would they think? How would they respond? Would they be jealous or afraid? My first task with my children was to educate them and provide for them a role model for coping with fear and anger in the context of the gospel mandate to show love and compassion. It was not easy. They had not yet met Larry.

The first time he came to our home we sat on the front porch and just talked. I should say talked and laughed and laughed and laughed some more. Laughter is powerful medicine and Larry had the wonderful gift of gab and humor, so his comedic style broke the ice with the girls, as well as afforded much spiritual healing for all of us. They grew to love him. There was no need to further persuade them into agreeing with what I had done.

Weeks went by. Larry became an important part of our family life. Everything Larry did was memorable and festive and we participated fully in every moment because we believed it would be Larry's last time to do it. Our lives would never be the same because of him. The more we all got to know and appreciate Larry's giftedness, the more I shook my head at the prospect that his own parents would never see or speak with him again. To me it was inconceivable. I was privileged to call Larry my son, and throughout the following months, my church people grew to love him as well, as he became more present in his healthier days. He even joined the choir and sang "O Holy Night" on Christmas Eve, an event tearfully and poignantly experienced by all.

Those days and months at First Church for Larry were not lived out in a "happily ever after" way simply because I had formed this unique relationship with him. There were countless times when we would try to contact his parents or other relatives, only to be ignored or have someone rudely hang up the phone. It was always a puzzle to me how this continued to be the case. I had hoped, as Larry did, that somehow, over time, his parents would soften and want to be there for him in a caring way, but they never did. But that became part of our association—the bond as well as the broken heart, always there in the background, as we dealt with the realities of rejection.

Most of the time, however, we had a life-giving relationship in which we both learned a lot. Larry is the one who helped me most to imagine what it is like to be gay. I felt so relaxed around him that I was able to put some of my most perplexing questions to him about being homosexual. I was filled with curiosity about how it felt to be gay, what he did, how he related, the problems it created with other people, and the discrimination he experienced because of it. Larry was so kind and patient with me. Some of my questions made him laugh out loud, but he always treated them with seriousness and the respect required to try to explain things to me. In the years since my encounter with John, I have recognized this as one of the most enlightening times of my life. My worldview took a quantum leap forward as he spelled things out for me. Larry needed me to be his mother and pastor, and I needed him to be my helper and teacher. It was a beautiful arrangement, which was surrounded by family and church in love and understanding.

After months of learning about homosexuality from Larry, I still had lifestyle questions based on old stereotypes that needed to be addressed, and so one day he offered me an unusual invitation. "Mama," he said, "I think it's time that I took you on a Gay Pittsburgh By Night Tour. You need to see what I'm talking about firsthand."

I didn't know what to think. How would it be to go into places where gay people were open about who they were? Would anyone try to flirt with me? What would I do? How could I let Larry know if I was uncomfortable, yet still be there for him in these places? What was it he wanted me to see? I would soon find out.

We started by going to a place that was once a very large house. It was Victorian in style, and the three floors had been redesigned into a drinking establishment with several separate bars. It was fairly early in the evening and not many people were there but Larry knew some of the folks and he got a big kick out of introducing me to them and the bartenders as his "Mom." We spent about twenty minutes there and then went downtown to a place that was really a nightclub with live music and dancing. There was special lighting and décor, which made it quite an upbeat and energetic place. Here it was much more crowded, although the hour was still early. About a dozen people were on the floor dancing to some rock music, and so Larry and I did this too. Most everyone on the dance floor was male, and it was the first time I had ever seen anything like this. When the lights lowered and the band played a slow song, same sex couples drifted to the floor and began to dance together. Larry and I sat and watched. I wasn't sure what I was seeing. It was too new. Yet I was struck by a certain natural quality in this scene, in spite of how strange it seemed to me. These people were so at home in this company. They seemed relaxed and safe, without fear of judgment or rude disclosure. I felt as if I had been transported into a parallel world of acceptance and affirmation.

After that we went to a place that looked like a warehouse. Outside were parked several motorcycles among the cars, and when we went inside, the bar was filled with men who were dressed in leather outfits. I was the only woman in the room, and again Larry took great delight in introducing me as "Mom." I never corrected that impression because it was fun to see the looks on peoples' faces as they tried to imagine how I could be Larry's mother. The most important thing was that Larry was so thoroughly pleased to be showing me around, meeting people he knew, and loving the idea that an affirming mother figure was accompanying him into his world.

After a while, Larry became a bit serious and told me that he wanted me to see something out in the back. We walked the full length of the room and then stepped out onto what appeared to be an old loading dock which spanned the whole back side of the building. There in the darkened walkway I saw a long row of mattresses lying side by side on the cement. No one was out there at the moment except the two of us, and at first I didn't comprehend what I was seeing. But slowly, the dawn of realization filled my mind's eye as I started to imagine what would happen in this place as the night progressed. I suddenly felt sick to my stomach and told Larry that I wanted to leave. I couldn't believe my eyes, and yet I was glad that we had gone there before anyone else was out there.

As we walked to the car and prepared to go to the next place my heart was troubled. An avalanche of questions tumbled into my mind and spirit, each one hanging in the darkness and demanding an answer as I contemplated this startling introduction into another aspect of gay life. Why did people come to places like this last one? What could they be looking for? How desperate and lonely would a person have to be to come to a bar with mattresses on the back porch? Was there no other place to meet someone? Was there no alternative that was wholesome and safe and provided value-centered relationships? I immediately thought of the church. Of course! The church purports to be such a place. Yet I also quickly realized that the church was probably the last place in the world that some of these people would look to get affirmation and acceptance. The church, with its traditional teachings about homosexuality, would condemn, admonish, and shun these people; it would probably not welcome them and encourage them to find healthy, stable relationships. It occurred to me that the church that criticizes some of the life-destroying behaviors in the gay community is the very church that is responsible, because of its judgments and criticisms, for alienating these people to the point where they have turned away from the church to these alternatives. Some straights are offended by gays when they behave in immoral and inappropriate ways, but where does the church teach them to do otherwise? The church has helped to create the very lifestyle that it condemns, by abandoning them in their need. Where then does the gay community find their moral guidelines? Who is there in the darkness among the bars and booze and mattresses to help these people find genuine, life-giving, loving relationships rather than one night stands?

The most urgent question coming from a place deep within the pain of my soul was "Where is the church? Where is it?" Are we so constrained and closed-minded in our attitudes toward homosexuality that we won't even look at the anguish of its community? How can we hope to bring a word of grace to people if we refuse to look beyond our own automatic sweeping judgments to see where their real yearnings are? How can we even claim to be the church if our own doctrine, on principle, turns people away without really listening to who they are and what their struggles may be? I didn't want to see any more. I wanted to go home. Something was forming in my spirit that would affect my ministry from that moment on. Larry must have seen that the experience had done something to me. We hardly spoke at all as he drove me home. I didn't know what to say. I barely knew what to think. As I got out of the car that night Larry hugged me and said, "What are you gonna do, Mama?"

"I don't know, son," I said quietly as I looked into his questioning eyes. "I don't know."

## From Hope to Hostility

It would be a long time before I would see a clear pathway to ministry based on my newly expanding worldview, which included greater understanding and experience of the gay community. Meanwhile, I was beginning to see more evidence within my own church that such ministry was needed. It happened that, in the course of preparing the AIDS seminar, there were a few men in my congregation who had put themselves into the task with their whole heart and soul. I had never thought of these particular men as ones who had special abilities or enthusiasm for educational endeavors, because they had previously stayed in the background of church life. I began to think about that and about these men. They were all single. They did not date women. All they shared in common was that they were compassionate and they gave countless hours to the cause. Could they be gay? The next several months would be very telling for me as I watched and listened for other clues.

It helped a lot to have Larry join our congregation and be "out" and active in the life of the church. These men were among the first to surround Larry with the community that he craved. It was Larry who broke the ice with one or two of them who came out to me. I was thankful for this, yet I also felt considerable sadness, because it seemed that the men had waited such a long time within their own community of faith to have that one opportunity to be open and honest about who they were. I had to tell myself "Better late than never" in order to deal with my feelings and recognize this as a truly positive step.

It was just a matter of time until our church became known as a place of trust and sanctuary for all types of persons. More of the gay men in the congregation came out to me, and they felt comfortable bringing their friends to the church. Once or twice a year we would offer a class on the subject of homosexuality, so that people could be educated and enter into dialogue about their feelings, and some of these same men would attend to take part in the discussion without coming out to the group. First Church was beginning to be a different kind of place, one that incorporated a more visible diversity and energy.

During that same period I was pursuing a doctoral program where, in the course of my studies, I was able to read several dozen books on the subject of homosexuality in preparation for my thesis (see the Appendix). It was in the course of this study that I became totally convinced that homosexuality is not a sin, nor is it unnatural for persons born with a non-heterosexual orientation. I concluded this from my reading, but even more from hearing the stories of the homosexual people who would come to me to talk and seek counsel.

CHAPTER 3

# Getting Bolder

*"Truth, divorced from experience,*
*will always dwell in the realm of doubt." —Henry Krause*

The summer that Larry died, I realized that my experiences had readied me to take some actions on behalf of sexual minorities. I knew also that this was no longer a choice for me, it was a calling, and I had to do it. It wasn't an easy realization, but one that followed my conscience: to be radically loving and inclusive—and to be willing to do so at the risk of being condemned and attacked by the institution that had deserted these people.

I made two decisions that helped to define my position in relation to mainstream Christian teaching: first, I would demonstrate my solidarity with gays by marching in the Pride Parade; second, I would attempt to reconcile my disputes with organized religion by initiating an ecumenical ministry with gays in Pittsburgh.

My determination to participate in the Pride Parade was the more difficult of the two decisions, and not something that occurred dispassionately. I had been invited to take part in the parade by a gay friend, and I discovered that I wasn't nearly prepared for the internal struggle that would ensue. To begin with, I didn't know what people might think if they saw me

27

walking in the Pride Parade. Suppose someone from my church saw me and assumed that I was gay? Suppose the media showed up with cameras and my face appeared on the evening news? Then the chances would be much greater that someone I knew would see me.

Perhaps I would wear sunglasses and a hat and stay behind one of the banners. Of course, I would position myself in one of the less conspicuous places in the middle. Maybe the best decision of all would be to stay home and politely explain that I had something else to do that morning.

Then something of my own doing brought the struggle unavoidably closer. I was scheduled to preach on the day after the parade and my sermon title had been on display for the entire week. The title was "Risky Business." It had to do with the risks we must sometimes take in order to stand up for what we believe. I was nailed. My own sermon would condemn me if I did not walk with the others. How could I, in good conscience, urge people to take risks for the sake of the gospel if I myself was unwilling to do so? I had no other choice. I would walk in the Pride Parade.

When the day finally arrived, I drove downtown to the announced gathering place. I pulled into the parking lot near the Civic Arena just as it began to rain. "Oh, great," I said to myself. "On top of everything else, I have to do this in the rain!"

I waited in my car as long as I possibly could before getting out onto the crowded pavement to find the people I knew. There were all kinds of folks milling around, and slowly there seemed to be some order to the thing. Banners helped to identify the groups. My eyes searched the sea of faces and flags to find my friend, and then I hurried to join him. The rain had lessened to a slight drizzle as we stood waiting for the sun to appear from behind the storm cloud overhead.

As I approached, I had a chance to really look around and see who else was taking part that day. Lots of different groups representing aspects of gay life in Pittsburgh were participating, including about a thousand people from agencies, clubs, sports groups, university organizations and a supportive group called PFLAG (Parents and Friends of Lesbians and Gays). There were rainbow flags and pink triangles everywhere as symbols of gay pride. Many people wore T-shirts with slogans on them such as "I can't even THINK straight," or "Hate is not a family value," or "Teach Tolerance." Some of the more flamboyant men were wearing leather peek-a-boo shorts and tops and were going out of their way to kiss each other in front of the TV cameras. There were even men, riding on the back of shiny convertibles, who were dressed as beautiful women in evening gowns and wigs. However, most of the people I saw looked very ordinary and a few of them looked pretty scared.

As the parade moved from the uptown section down through the city streets, police officers were there to block the intersections from any traffic. Several hundred people had lined the streets on both sides as we wound our way past the department stores, office buildings, and businesses. By then, the rain had stopped and shoppers could stop to see this strange sight passing by. Some of the marching groups had chants or songs that they were singing as we walked. The crowd immediately behind me was young and full of energy and fun. They walked in cadence and kept shouting, "Two, four, six, eight: how d'ya know your kid is straight?" Their antics helped everyone to get into the pride spirit.

But not everyone who stood by and watched was happy with this demonstration. Some office workers looked down from the glass windows up above, coffee cups in hand while pointing and jeering. Once in awhile someone along the way would yell some obscenity and send a rude gesture our way. As we went further and further along toward Point State Park, I began to understand what this kind of pride was all about. It was saying, "Here we are. We are proud of who we are, and we are not going to deny it anymore. We are standing tall, side by side with our brothers and sisters because we love them and we feel their pain. We join together to do this so that we might give courage to each other and to others who are not yet able to walk with us."

When we finally arrived at the park, there was a stage set up for the speeches to be given by various leaders in the gay community. It was a very affirming time. We all sat down in the wet grass together—old, young, black, white, Asian, male, female, gay, straight, bisexual, and transgendered. We truly made a community together as we listened to words of hope and challenge. It was wonderful. I was aware of only four or five clergy in all this crowd.

As I looked around, I understood that I was quite a fool in my struggle about whether or not to walk. My biggest fear was that someone might think I was gay, yet here were several hundred beautiful men and women who were in fact gay or belonged to a sexual minority, and it was they, much more than I, who showed courage in what they risked that day. They were jeopardizing their family ties, their jobs, even their friends, at a much deeper, more consequential level than I, and even threatening the assurance of their housing and personal safety.

Each time I experienced a new facet of life in the gay community, I seemed to feel a greater kinship with those who are living through the pressures of being part of a sexual minority. The Pride events were informative for me. Not long afterward, I was led to my second major decision of the summer: to explore the idea of an ecumenical ministry to and with gays.

I remembered the mattresses on the back porch of that downtown bar. I thought about the Pride Parade that helped empower larger numbers of people gathering together for courage and support. I recalled the rich sense of fellowship shared by the gay men in my congregation. Suppose the church could provide a safe venue where persons could come (without the pressure and atmosphere of a bar) to meet others and find healthy relationships? Could this be one hopeful alternative that the church could offer?

After a couple of months of planning, refining, recruiting, and scheduling, GLAD (Gay and Lesbian Alternative Dimensions) was born. It was to be group for gay, lesbian, bisexual, and transgendered persons, with eight sponsoring clergy agreeing to take turns hosting social events at our churches, which would include opening devotions, a program, and a time of refreshments. A kickoff dance was scheduled to take place at First Church. We passed out flyers about GLAD at a gay community picnic where several hundred people were milling around in the park. A lot of them came to see what we had to offer, and some of the reactions of various people were quite dramatic.

Most of the folks were very friendly. Occasionally someone would say, "This is a *church*-related group?" and seemed amazed and delighted that church and gay activities could possibly go together. Still others would see what we had given them and suddenly become upset. The flyer would then be angrily torn up and thrown down in disgust by a person who seemingly had been severely embittered and alienated by religion. Apparently there were some people at one extreme who had come to feel that God was the only one left who could profoundly love and understand them; and at the other extreme were those who could not, would not, worship a God who so harshly judged and punished them. When I saw the mix of emotions on the faces of those in the park who were offered an open door to a community of faith, I was even more convinced that the church could certainly meet a very special and profound need.

It appears that this determination was correct. We welcomed almost seventy-five gay, lesbian, and bisexual persons to that first dance and social hour. It was great. It was solid. People were having a good time. They were laughing and dancing and gathering together in small groups to joke and talk. It felt like a bold new statement was being proclaimed in the gay community: "Here is a place where you are safe, loved, and accepted, just as you are." I looked around the room and saw men and women, younger and older, who could have been my brother, my daughter, my co-worker, or my uncle. These were ordinary people in every way, even in their yearning for the affirmation that comes with the freedom to be who they really are. And to think, this was happening in a church, with the support and sponsorship of several congregations.

Some of the comments I heard at that first gathering were, "It's really hard for me to know where to go to meet nice people. I don't drink, and so I don't like to go to bars. This is the perfect place." Or, "My friends at school are in Act Up or Cry Out, but that just isn't me. I'm pretty quiet and don't want to make a big deal out of anything. So this is just the right kind of place for me to get involved." Or, "I *never* thought I'd be accepted in a church! This is fantastic!"

That first small step was the beginning of some of the most meaningful ministry of my entire career. Over the next three years more pastors and congregations would participate at some level in this new venture. A bold new challenge would continue to come forth from the gay-friendly religious community. More and more lives would be touched so that healing could begin between mind and spirit. Support groups would be formed, deep friendships would be made, and I would meet and hear the stories of scores and scores of people trapped in the struggle between sexuality and spirituality.

PART II

# Sharing
# the
# Struggle

CHAPTER 4

# Meeting the People

A young woman walks into a pastor's office because she wants to know if she is going to hell for being homosexual. Now, aside from any theological discussion that might take place regarding the literal existence of places called heaven and hell, much of the conversation between the woman and the pastor will probably center around the compatibility of homosexuality and the practice of it with Christian teaching. The tragedy of this scene is that the pastor, most likely straight and representative of the majority mainline point of view, will probably counsel her to try to be converted to heterosexuality, or—if that seems impossible—to try to remain celibate for the rest of her life; for after all, the church loves the "sinner" but not the "sin." And so the courage that the young woman found to first enter the portals of the pastor's study may have been mustered in vain as she now must make some crucial choices that will redefine her relationship with many persons in many settings, including the church. This scenario happens many times every day across Christendom, and many of the pastors involved have nothing but scripture, tradition, and reason to help answer questions such as these. They have not heard the experiences of persons who are different sexually, whose truth presents difficulties that are not shared openly in the mainstream church, experiences that can help all of us to understand the struggles of the person of faith who happens to be gay, lesbian, bisexual, or transgendered.

Here are twelve stories of men and women who represent glimpses of real life in the sexual minority community. It is these experiences, plus what I learned in sharing these experiences, that brings church teachings about the practice of homosexuality into question. They are persons who have hopes and dreams, fears and feelings just as any person would have. The issues they struggle with are similar to anyone's, except that these people are embodied differently, making the traditional moral code of the church irrelevant in many ways.

Some of the people in these stories have had dealings with the church in a direct way, others have not. The reason these stories are important and included, however, is that they represent persons who are in our congregations right now, living their lives, with or without the support of the church. What would happen in your congregation if one of these people would want to share such an experience with you? Would they be welcomed, accepted, loved, celebrated? Or would they have to look outside the church for what they most need to get from people of faith? The answer to these questions will define us as a church.

The stories represent a microcosm—a spectrum of real, everyday experience—that is probably very different from your own. I only ask that as you read these stories, you attempt to really see and hear the pastoral issues that attend these experiences and that you try to suspend judgment (based on other criteria) until these stories have been incorporated into your awareness. Otherwise, these representative persons and millions like them remain silent in our dealings with them. They will have no reason to relate to us with such authenticity and sincerity unless we open our eyes and ears and hearts in a new way.

Think of the people in these stories not just as examples across the spectrum of sexual identity—think of them too, as neighbors, as friends, as family members, for they are that. And think of them, while you read, as churchgoers who love God and seek what each of us is seeking—a spiritual connection to God in mutual fellowship with other Christians.

Some of what you read may trouble you, leave you frustrated and uneasy. The stories may be difficult to read. They may challenge you, and you may not know what to do with your feelings. But life does that, and this is real life.

Let us hear these real ways of living from folks who exist with very different maps of reality—*not by choice*, but by nature and painful discovery. By sharing some of these stories, I hope that more people of faith will come to understand the struggle that sexual minorities live with every day, a struggle that is often heightened by the negative voice of religion; a voice that instead should be in the forefront of healing and love. Each situation will show us in some manner how the church has not been there in positive ways at formative and arduous times in these person's lives, most often because of our preoccupation with matters of legalism. Perhaps you, after reading these stories, will begin to ask with me how the church can be more than welcoming to persons who feel so excluded from its fellowship. How can we learn to be loving and affirming?

The names of all persons have been changed to protect them from unwanted disclosure because of their sexual orientation. Some of these persons represent composites of more than one story that typifies experience in the gender minority community.

## CHAPTER 5

# Pastor Problems:
# Nicholas, Lisa, and Rich

*"Biblical orthodoxy without compassion*
*is surely the ugliest thing in the world."*
—Francis A. Schaeffer

## Nicholas

*Nicholas thought he could trust his pastor, until...*

"Reverend Waun," said a quiet voice at the other end of the phone. "You don't know me, but I visited your church last Sunday and I really need to come and talk with you. It's...it's a personal matter. A friend of mine said you might be able to help."

"Sure," I said, "I'd be glad to talk with you," and we set up a time. When Nicholas arrived at my door he impressed me immediately as one who carried the weight of the world on his shoulders. He was a man in his mid-thirties who was exceptionally handsome, who could have carried off a fairly high level of confidence based on looks alone, yet there was a noticeable sadness about him. His black eyes looked as if they were holding back a deluge of tears, and his manner was dejected as he chose the chair in my office nearest the box of tissues. I watched him as he sat down and placed his hands calmly in his lap.

"What brings you here today?" I asked with a smile, hoping to put him at ease as I sat down in my rocking chair.

"I don't know where to begin," said Nicholas, looking down at his shoes. "I've just had a terrible fight with my parents and now my brother and his family are turned against me, too."

"What happened?" I asked gently. Nicholas' head dropped down into his hands and he sat there for a moment shaking it back and forth as if he couldn't believe what he was about to tell me.

"It's about my church," he said. "Well, I *thought* it was my church." He looked up. "It's been my church all my life. I went there as a child with my parents...my brother...I went to Sunday School there. That's where I learned about Jesus—and love. I was even baptized there..." his voice trailed off.

I was preparing myself for some wrenching tale of how Nicholas, his family, and his church have come to a new and unfortunate place of tension and pain. What could it be?

"Go on," I urged.

The young man in my office returned his gaze to his shoes, shaking his head again.

"I've been working really hard on myself. You know what I mean?" He glanced at me momentarily and then back down. "I...well...I've been in therapy for quite sometime, trying to come to terms with the fact that I'm gay. I always knew there was something different about me—ever since I was a kid. I never really liked girls, but my folks wanted me to, so I dated a few times in high school."

Nicholas began picking at the hangnail on one thumb with the nail of his other thumb—soft, clicking jabs of nervous energy. He looked up at me like a child, seeking approval. I nodded my head at him silently.

"Anyway," he continued, "it wasn't until years later that I wondered if I might be gay and went to a counselor about it." That was about four years ago, and right now I've never felt stronger in terms of who I am. I know that I really am gay. At first, I was scared to death, because I didn't want to be gay. Who would *want* to be gay? Who would *choose* this? I thought about my family and about what they might say, but I knew I'd have to tell them sometime."

Nicholas' voice picked up a firmer tone as he talked about these recent insights. It was plain to see that he had gained some resolve around not backing down from his gay identity. He was clearly defending his boundary there. Yet how, I wondered, did this get him into trouble with the church?

"One day," said Nicholas, "I decided to have a talk with my Dad. He's really the one in my family who's easiest to talk to. I figured that if I could find a way to tell Dad I'm gay, telling Mom and my brother would be easier...or maybe Dad would be the one to pave the way for me. Anyway, I thought I would start with him."

"How did it go?" I asked.

"Well, actually, it went pretty well," he explained. "He just sat and listened. He didn't say much. He didn't ask me any questions...oh well, except, 'You don't have AIDS, do you?'"

Nicholas seemed peeved at the memory of his dad's question.

"But he didn't get angry or anything. He told me right away *not* to tell Mom. He was sure she would freak out. So I just let it go for a long time. At least it was a beginning. Since then, I've been with my family for a couple of holidays, and once I even took Brad along (he's my partner)..." Nicholas looked at me briefly to see how I would react. I didn't. "They were nice enough to us but they never wanted to talk about anything serious. I guess the rule at that time was: Don't talk about being gay and we'll pretend everything's fine."

"Does your mom know now?" I asked.

"Well," he replied with a pained look. "She sure does. My whole family knows, and we have these big fights about it all the time. Look," said Nicholas, sitting straight up in his chair, "here's what happened a couple of months ago."

I sensed he was getting closer to the real reason he had come to see me that day.

"It was harder and harder to keep the fact that I'm gay from other people in my life, so I decided to go to my pastor about this...to see if he had any advice for me."

It was as though the remembrance of that decision made him feel stupid for ever thinking that it might help. He punctuated his sentence with a thrust of his hand, and then slumped his head down again.

His voice broke. "I can't believe what happened. I was honest with him. I told him everything...about realizing I was gay...and about how I told my Dad...and about how my mom didn't know yet because of how mad she'd be..." Nicholas reached for a tissue. "I wanted him to know how hard this was for me because I love my family...I've always been close to my family...and I...well...I just needed him to help me know what to do, and maybe to pray with me."

Nicholas could no longer contain himself. The tears began to trickle down his cheeks. I reached out and put my hand on his knee. When he felt my touch, he simply collapsed into sobbing.

I sat with steady pressure from my hand on his knee while he cried and buried his eyes in a very wet tissue. Finally, he looked up to recount the next part of his story. I sat back to listen.

"About a week later," he said, "I was sitting in my living room...It was about seven o'clock at night. I had just finished watching the evening news. I heard a car pull into my driveway, and I got up to look out the window, to see who it was. There was a black van out there, and six men got out and came up onto my porch. The doorbell rang. I answered it, and the first person I saw was my pastor...the same one I had gone to see."

The scene I pictured as he spoke was like something out of an Elliot Ness movie. Was this real life?

"The pastor asked me if they could come in. They wanted to have a talk with me. Well, I didn't know what it was about, but I invited them in. I thought maybe it had something to do with getting me to raise my contribution to the church. Why would six men from the church come to my house?"

I was wondering the same thing.

"The pastor said I was their brother in Christ and that they were all really concerned about me. He had *told* all of them...those men who were there, who were elders in the church...he had told them everything I had told *him*."

Aside from the blatant breaking of the trust and confidentiality that Nicholas had placed in him, this pastor had shown the audacity to bring elders of the church into Nicholas' own home to confront him in a perverse intrusion.

All I could say to Nicholas was, "Oh my God."

"They sat and talked with me for about an hour. They told me that if I chose to be gay, that I would have to leave the church, because I was not welcome there. But…if I gave up being gay, they would let me stay and they would help me to resist temptation. I tried to tell them that I didn't *choose* to be gay…it is who I am, and that if I have to change to be welcome in my own church, then I couldn't do it."

Nicholas' thumbnail was picking away again.

"They told me they loved me and they wanted to pray for me because they didn't want me to go to hell." The look on Nicholas' face said it all—he had been absolutely demolished by this encounter. No wonder he seemed to be burdened by the weight of the world. I couldn't imagine such a horrible meeting with fellow Christians who came purporting to bring the love of Christ. Where was the love now? Where was the healing, the hope? I supposed that the fact that he was sitting at the moment in my office—the office of a church pastor—was at least one small sign that he had not entirely given up trust or hope in the church—or, at least, in God. That was the one small realization that sustained me.

Nicholas continued. "I listened to everything they had to say, and then I asked them, 'Who makes the final decision about whether I withdraw my membership or not?' They said, 'You do.' And I said, 'Well then, I'm not leaving! You'll have to put up with me!'" The strong tone had come back into Nicholas' voice.

"Did you stay?" I asked.

Nicholas shook his head. "How could I ever go back after that?" he posed.

I knew that he was right. How could he go back after such treatment? By now, the elders would have told everyone else in the congregation, and they would be waiting for Nicholas to walk through the door. And when he did, they would have plenty of judgments for him. Why would he set himself up for such an ordeal? The thought that these well-meaning Christian people would do more to hurt than to heal was repulsive to me. The fights Nicholas had been having with his family were over the fact that their pastor had also shared everything Nicholas had said in confidence with them as well, and of course they were siding with the pastor and leaders of their church. Even more, they were insisting that Nicholas give up this silly stubbornness once and for all.

"How can I help?" I asked.

"I've been thinking," he said. "It's been six months since that happened. I never went back to my church again. But I want to go to church. It's part of who I am. I still believe in God…and I need to be around faithful people who can love me as I am…and not discount me or make me change. I've worked too hard on myself to settle for less."

I smiled at the confidence I continued to hear as Nicholas spoke about his selfhood. I was relieved that Nicholas was willing to stick up for his own relationship with God, even if his pastor had challenged it.

"I was wondering," he said, "if I could join this church. Would I be allowed to do that?"

"Of course," I replied. "You can join our next membership class."

"What about my other church?" he asked.

"Don't worry about that," I reassured him. "All we have to do is write for a letter of transfer and after you officially join, we add your name to our roll."

Nicholas looked relieved. I ended our time together with a prayer of thanksgiving for Nicholas and his faithfulness to God. Later, when it was time to write to the pastor of his church, I decided to do it myself, with a personal letter from me to him, explaining that we now have this beautiful child of God who has come to us wanting to join our church, bringing his wonderful gifts and graces, and that we accept him thankfully. My hope was that the letter would raise the consciousness of that pastor and the others who had been so condemning and cruel. The reality is, however, that they were probably not the least bit dissuaded from their position by my letter. In fact, I suspect that in addition to praying for Nicholas' eternal salvation, those stern and dutiful church people were also praying for mine. What a joy it is now, whenever I see Nicholas involved in some aspect of the life of our church, to notice the happy sparkle in his black eyes.

## Lisa

*Her pastor had been a best friend growing up, but now...*

Like Nicholas, a woman named Lisa was also struggling with the pastor of her church, but the difference is, that pastor didn't even know it. "My dilemma," she shared, "is that my pastor has been a close personal friend...all my life. We grew up together in that church. We were cutups together in Sunday School. We were even part of the 'Gassers' in Youth Club. That means we could all belch on demand and crack up the whole group."

I smiled because the description she offered of herself as a teenager was in such contrast with the person who sat before me now.

She bubbled on, "We could share our deepest secrets with each other...and—believe me—we had quite a few. Especially when we started dating."

Lisa was an attractive businesswoman in her late twenties, with light brown hair, hazel eyes, and a trim figure. She took care of herself by exercising and playing in a softball league. Everything about her seemed carefully thought out—the way the colors of her clothes, accessories, and makeup matched, the way she set career goals, the way she gathered information to make important decisions. She had come to see me to talk about one significant choice that she was wanting to make: should she come out to her pastor?

This was not an easy matter. Ron, her long-time friend, was now the pastor of her home church—he preached, taught, and led the people in attitude and spirit. Lisa had been trying to determine where Ron stood on the issue of homosexuality, based on his sermons and other comments. So far, it seemed that he was pretty conservative, from what she could observe.

"So, why do you want to tell him?" I asked.

Lisa was calm and confident. "I'm tired of lying about who I am to the most important community I have (outside my family): my church." She said this as though she was absolutely convinced of this, yet her emotions hadn't caught up with her words. It was clear that she was in great turmoil about this decision.

"Tell me about your church friends," I said. Lisa smiled. It seemed obvious that she delighted in the subject.

"Well," she began, "these are some wonderful people. They are friendly and attentive to me and think of me as a daughter. They are always really glad to see me and very much interested in my life."

At this point, Lisa hesitated, as if something in the background of what she was saying had just pushed through and caused her to frown. She was feeling the conflict she was about to describe to me.

"I've met someone," explained Lisa. "It's the first time in my life I've felt this way about anyone, and I'm just bursting to share it with my friends at church." She gestured to an imaginary place behind her. "I want to shout it to the world," she announced, beaming. But the frown quickly returned. "I don't know what would happen if I told the folks at church," she pondered. "I suppose some of them would think it was neat, and some others would never speak to me again. It would change everything…but still, there's a huge part of my life that they don't even know about. I want them to know everything about me…I want them to accept me for who I really am, not who I pretend to be, or who they *think* I am," she said with resolve.

"And you thought you'd tell Ron in order to test this out?" I asked.

"Yes," she replied with a smile.

I wanted to encourage her to fantasize the consequences of her various choices. "Suppose you tell Ron and he rejects you or tells you that you have to change, or uses this information against you somehow," I cautioned, remembering what had happened to Nicholas. "How would you handle that?"

Lisa nodded her head. "I've thought of that," she said. "I thought maybe Ron would take a different, more open attitude with me, since we've been friends for so long. I can't imagine that he would condemn me like someone he didn't even know. He would try to understand me, wouldn't he?" Lisa's eyes pleaded with me.

I wanted to share with Lisa some of the horrible scenes I could imagine, based on well-intentioned actions of other Christians I had heard about in similar situations, but I didn't want to overwhelm her with discouragement.

"You can't be sure of that, Lisa," I said finally. "Ron is in a position of leadership and authority now. He's formed opinions and teaches in certain ways based on what he's read and what he believes." I tried not to be too negative, but I did want Lisa to know that childhood friends can desert us if we find ourselves in opposite camps as adults. I think this is the kind of honesty Lisa was looking for. She had come here to think through all the consequences and gather all the information she could before deciding what to do about this. I admired her self-determination.

Self-determination aside, the lingering question that Lisa, and others like her, bring to light is the agony of whether one can be totally honest and risk rejection from the very church family that brings comfort and nurture. If not, one must hide a very significant part of life at the expense of personal integrity and full acceptance. I wondered how Lisa and Nicholas and others were able to do it.

## Rich

*What sort of minefield was God asking him to cross...*

Rich represents another sort of problem with the pastoral role. This young man came to see me after several years of involvement in my church. He is a warm, energetic people-person who knows how to give hugs and compliments and words of comfort and encouragement to those around him. He has a heart for missions and often helps with church projects. When Rich made an appointment to talk, I had a hunch that he wanted to tell me that he is gay, but I wasn't prepared for what he would describe.

"Renee," he began (my friends call me Renee), "I need to get your advice about some things." He seemed eager to share what was on his mind. "You see," he said assuredly, "I've known for about three years that I'm gay." He said this so matter-of-factly that I knew this was not the issue that brought him to my office.

"My partner Tim and I have talked about this a lot lately, and it was partly his idea that I come here today." In a few short moments Rich had come out to me and told me he had a partner. But there was still more.

"Renee," Rich asked, his eyes wide with excitement, "what does it feel like to be called to ministry?"

A person who asks such a question is usually one who *is* feeling called to ministry. I was thrilled. Of course, Rich would make an extraordinary pastor. He was considerably talented. He loved people and people loved him. His heart was moved to compassion for those in need, and Rich knew how to get things done. What a wonderful revelation.

Those were my first thoughts. My second thoughts plunged me into a backwash of feelings. "Oh my God," I realized, "Rich could never be ordained in this church. We have a ruling that excludes self-avowed, practicing gays from the ministry." What could I say to Rich? How could I possibly advise him? I suddenly saw the whole path that he would have to walk, laid out before him. Did I have the heart to break it to him?

My mind's eye took me back to my interview with John and then to angry comments by some of my own clergy colleagues in speaking against the ordination of gays.

"Tell me about your call to ministry," I said. Rich's face lit up as he sat up in his chair, eager to share.

"I guess it happened here at First Church," he said, bubbling with excitement.

He went on to tell me of the deep sense of satisfaction that he would get when he was engaged in a mission activity. He said that it seemed as if God was suggesting to him in each setting, "Yes, this is where I want you to be. This will be your work. I will lead you to places of greater work and ministry." Rich stopped, letting those words sink in as if the voice of God had just been in the room speaking again to affirm the calling he was feeling.

I knew that the church searched a person's life for signs of call, both internal and external, meaning that Rich himself must feel a sense of call, in addition to it being outwardly visible to others who would validate it. I saw both of these signs in Rich's story, yet what would Rich do when he started through the multistep process that would take him before boards and committees who would ask him all sorts of questions, possibly about his personal life? Suppose someone came right out and asked him if he were a practicing homosexual? Or what if, as happened in

John's case, someone guessed it and confronted him? I posed these questions to Rich. Would he want to admit this? He seemed instantly deflated. The excitement with which he described his call was gone, replaced by a kind of doleful countenance. He seemed to be searching for what to say next.

I had already concluded that this exceptional candidate for ministry would have only one decision to make before he could pursue his call. "Rich," I ventured, "the way I see things, you have to decide up front whether or not you want to be open about being gay. Everything else gets decided after that."

I sat back and waited several moments for Rich to speak. He had folded his hands and lifted them to tap both thumbs against his chin as he studied the stained glass window in my office that says, "Be ye doers of the word, and not hearers only" (James 1:22, KJV).

Finally he spoke softly. "Suppose I want to be a mainstream pastor—what do I do?" His eyes turned toward me, hands still folded.

"In most of them you have to withhold your sexual identity," I responded.

Rich extended his forefingers upward and pressed them to his lips. "Oh," he breathed dejectedly.

"There are other denominations where you wouldn't have to hide or lie," I hastened. I went on to describe the Metropolitan Community Church and the Unitarian Universalist Church, both of which have openly gay pastors.

When Rich heard that the MCC served largely gay congregations and that the UUC was not necessarily Christian, he was torn. "I want to serve a Christian congregation," he retorted, "and I want to be in a place where you find all kinds of people—gay, straight, old, young, black, white, families, couples—I don't want to specialize. To me, a community of faith has all of that variety in it. That's what I want...and I want to be open and honest about my orientation."

Rich seemed close to tears. This exuberant, eager young man who had come to me to share one of his most exciting spiritual experiences was now discouraged at the roadblocks I was identifying. It didn't seem fair. I felt that I, as a pastor, was the very one to blame for destroying his enthusiasm.

Here I was with one of the most talented, ideal persons that I could possibly imagine in the ordained ministry, called by God, yet he was stuck because his own denomination could not, would not ordain him if he were honest about his sexuality. I questioned again in my mind what one's sexual orientation could ever have to do with a person's relationship to the God who calls us, or what it could have to do with one's ability to serve a church. Why couldn't my own denomination accept Rich the way he is?

How could Rich be feeling about his position at the moment? He had just shared a high moment of call with his pastor, and was told that he would have to go to another denomination for fulfillment; at least, if he wanted to maintain his authenticity. It simply wasn't fair.

"You know, Rich," I began, "you're going to think this is bizarre, but do you know what I hope will happen?"

"What's that?" he asked, tilting his head slightly and frowning, as if he sensed my ambivalence.

"I hope if another denomination works out and you get serious about your call, that when it's time for you to leave our church, people here will find out why. And when they do, there'll be such an outcry of injustice on your behalf that maybe, just maybe, there'll be a movement for change that starts right here in our own congregation. The people here who know you, and love you, and will support your call to ministry—they're the most likely ones to want to change this absurd system. Maybe their righteous indignation will move someone around here to action. That's the only thing that will redeem this travesty for me."

Rich was very reflective. "Renee," he said quietly—suddenly he was *my* pastor—"God will work this out. If this is God's idea, God will find me a way to do this." He smiled and touched my hand. "It won't matter what denomination I serve, as long as I can pursue this call."

I knew he was right. I would do everything I could to help him find the right people, the next steps. I would help him to walk through the institutional minefields he would encounter. The most frustrating part was that I wanted to shout to the whole church what was going on behind the scenes, what Rich was struggling with, what the limited choices were for him. Yet I couldn't break his confidence. One day, Rich would go away and people would wonder why. Only then would there be the possibility that the information might be shared, with Rich's permission. I hoped that the aftermath would be life-giving for everyone.

CHAPTER 6

# Struggles in Coming Out:
# Karen, Bob, and Charlene

*"Love makes everything lovely;*
*hate concentrates on the one thing hated."*
—George MacDonald

Because traditional church teaching is that homosexuality is unnatural, persons who are gay, lesbian, bisexual, or transgendered are often delayed in realizing or accepting their orientation. The following three people may or may not have had a desire to be part of a community of faith. That is not their issue. It is their processes of coming out that show us that gay men and lesbians have the same emotions, needs, and desires as any one of us would have. If the church would advocate for being supportive throughout the coming out process, the world would be a safer, saner place in which sexual minorities could make themselves known.

## Karen
*She would rather die than tell her brother...*
Karen was a lesbian who regularly attended one of the support groups in our parish for people of faith who are coming out. Her

ongoing predicament was that she dearly loved her brother, his wife, and their twelve-year-old son, but she was convinced that if they knew she was a lesbian, they would have nothing to do with her. She was especially distraught to think that she might be barred from any relationship with her nephew. Karen had been married once and had a grown son of her own (who accepted her as a lesbian), but she felt she could not be honest with her own brother.

"Why not?" someone in the group would ask. "How do you know that your brother would end your relationship?"

"I just know it in my gut," Karen would answer.

"But how? How do you know?" would come the question.

"Well," Karen might say, "I just know from times I've been there when the subject came up around a TV show or a movie discussion. I can tell by his comments and his wife's that they would throw me out of their lives if I came out to them."

What this meant, of course, is that Karen had to hide a very significant part of her life from her family. Conversations tended to revolve around safe topics, where Karen would be quite certain that she would not have to reveal anything. She had to watch what she said because, even though she lived alone, her personal life was full of activity centered in the les/bi/gay/t (lesbian/bisexual/gay/transgendered) community, and she never shared any of the content or the meaning of it with them. It was always a sad and frustrating time for this support group who wanted so much to see Karen enjoy openness and freedom to be herself with those whom she loved so much, but we could never seem to help her with this.

One day we were shocked and grieved to learn that Karen had died suddenly. She was found on the floor of her kitchen by another friend who attended our support group. Devastated by this news, many of us prepared to go to the funeral home for the visitation.

Because Karen had been so extensively involved in the sexual minority community through group leadership and volunteer activities, there was a huge crowd of people there to pay respects. As we lined up to greet the family, I realized that there, waiting to shake my hand, was Karen's brother, his wife, and their twelve-year-old son. They were absorbed in their grief, and Karen's death was only half of it.

As people came through the line, the brother would ask each one how she or he had known Karen. When I overheard this, I wondered what I would say when it was my turn to shake his hand—that Karen was a regular attender of a support group for sexual minorities? How could I? This was the same brother and family for whom Karen's lesbian identity was a solid, well-kept secret. Would I unwittingly "out" her even as she lay in her coffin? I simply smiled and said, "Karen and I did some ecumenical projects together."

"Oh," he replied as he squeezed my hand. "Thank you for coming."

The next day, after the funeral, someone who was both a friend of Karen's brother and a support group member called me. We reflected on how many people who loved Karen attended the visitation. At the same time, he told me how, through the course of the whole unfortunate event, the brother and his family had come to realize that Karen was, in fact, a lesbian.

"How did they feel about that news?" I asked.

"They are in a state of disbelief, on top of everything else," he said.

"I wonder," I said, as I thought about the grieving couple, "how they would feel about coming to our next support group meeting. You know, it would be immensely helpful for us to hear their side of how Karen's identity was perceived by them. I would think it would also be useful to them as they work through this horrible time."

"I like the idea," said my friend. "I don't know how they'll feel about it. They're really upset by all this. But I'll give them a call and see. We probably shouldn't be too disappointed if they decide not to come."

"I know," I said. "But I think it's worth a try."

The most amazing thing is that the brother and his wife did come to our next meeting. It was a moment of privilege for all of us. There were those in the group who hadn't yet heard that Karen was dead and had to cope with the situation right then and there. Among them were two women who had taken Karen aside after the last meeting to continue their discussion in private about her situation with her brother. And here, at the very next meeting, they found out the dreadful news about Karen, at the same time we all sat together with her brother and his wife, who looked stunned and drained. It was intense.

"Tell us," I began, "about your relationship with Karen over the past few years."

The brother spoke softly. "Karen has always been a good sister," he said. "We were always very close growing up. After we both got married and had kids, our families would get together a lot. We all got along very well...had a lot of wonderful times." His eyes were red.

"Did you ever suspect that she was a lesbian?" I asked.

"No," he said simply. His wife sat in silence.

"How do you feel about this news now?" I asked. The others in the group were unusually still.

"I've been thinking about that a lot since Karen died," he said. "I have to say that I'm strangely relieved."

"How so?" I asked.

"Well, you see, something changed in our relationship with Karen. I guess it was about six years ago." The brother's wife nodded in agreement.

"It seemed to us like she was pulling back...like there was this strange sense of distance between us. We couldn't understand it. We had the feeling that Karen wasn't really with us any more...she wouldn't talk about her personal life as much. My wife and I discussed this a lot. We couldn't think of anything that we had done to cause this." The wife had started to cry softly.

"And so you're relieved because..." I offered.

"Because now we know for sure that it wasn't us at all...it was that she knew she was a lesbian and didn't want us to know it."

"In retrospect," I said, "how would you have felt had Karen come out to you then?"

The brother shifted his weight, offering an ever-so-slight break in the tension of the group, who waited eagerly to hear his reply.

"Well, to be perfectly honest," he said, "I wouldn't have wanted to hear that. We were brought up to believe that homosexuality is a sin. I probably would've denied it or been upset with her. But I would've gotten over it. At this point, what would

I rather have…a dead sister who can't be with us ever again, or a live sister who happens to be a lesbian? I wish she were alive and trusted me enough to share that part of herself with me. I guess it was my fault that she didn't feel comfortable enough to talk with me about it." Tears began to trickle down the brother's cheeks, and his wife leaned over to hug him.

It was an occasion that the group will long remember. It was a healing time for all of us, and one that meant all the more to a grieving family because of the openness of this faith community, which was there to receive them with compassion and understanding. This type of ministry is vital—and could be even more so, if the church as a whole were to re-examine its traditional teachings on homosexuality. If Karen's family had not been taught that homosexuality is a sin, she might have revealed her identity to them years ago and enjoyed a new level of sharing and mutual appreciation—while she was still alive. Why should honesty come with such an enormous price tag? It shouldn't, but when you're gay, it often does.

## Bob

*His tragedy was being "out" in the wrong place at the wrong time…*

The price of honesty was excruciating for a young man named Bob. It had been two years before he was able to talk about it, and the pain oozed out from behind every word. Perhaps Bob was suffering from a version of Post-Traumatic Stress Syndrome, where memories of an event too horrible to keep in the conscious mind were stuffed away somewhere into his subconscious, causing unpredictable panic attacks, nightmares, and flashbacks. For some reason, Bob was ready to talk about his experience with me.

Bob was a soft-spoken man in his early thirties whose manner was one of caring and gentleness. He told me how he had not known he was gay until his late twenties, when he finally confronted some nagging suspicions that he was having about himself. He had wondered why he was not interested in women, but he thought perhaps he was simply the shy type (which he was). The thought that he might be gay terrified him, and he postponed this consideration as long as he could. He buried himself in his work at a bank, working many extra hours on evenings and weekends. However, he was taken off-guard one day.

"I saw him for the first time in that little bookstore on Fifth Avenue," Bob said. "I just happened to be in there looking for a book about hummingbirds for my mother, when he appeared beside me in the aisle way. I never thought I believed in love at first sight until that moment," he said, in a manner that confused me, because his voice and demeanor was grief-stricken rather than elated, so I sat in silence, waiting for him to continue.

"I realized all at once," said Bob, taking a deep breath, "that my worst fear was true—I am gay." The bittersweet nature of this discovery was plain to see. He didn't want to be gay, but he longed for someone to love, and when the possibility presented itself, it was his worst nightmare, while at the same time, he was flooded with a kind of vitality he had never known before. It must have been frightening and wonderful all at the same time to meet a person—a man, not a woman—that could evoke these kinds of feelings in him.

"What did you do?" I asked.

Bob smiled impishly. "I happened to notice that he was carrying a copy of *In The Kitchen With Rosie*—that's the cookbook written by Oprah Winfrey's live-in cook," he explained.

I nodded.

"Anyway, I made some comment about that, just to have something to say." It seemed that an introvert like Bob would have to use considerable energy to think of something to say to a perfect stranger and then to risk saying it.

"He smiled at me," Bob said, dropping for a moment his sadness, to experience a bit of delight at this memory. "He told me he was wanting to try her recipe for some special soup he liked. Said something about doing more vegetarian stuff. I don't remember much about the conversation," he added. "I just remember how terrific he looked in his jeans and muscle shirt. I think I would have talked about anything to get his attention. He was *so* handsome!" Bob said. "All I knew was that I didn't want this man to walk out of my life."

Each pleasurable memory seemed laden with an edge of sorrow. "His name was Ken," Bob said wistfully. I noted his use of the past tense.

"We actually stood and talked in the bookstore for about twenty minutes, and I could tell he was flirting with me, too. It was fantastic. I never had such an experience in my life," Bob said. "I knew that he wanted to be there with me and it just blew my mind!"

I wondered how a shy, fearful person like Bob would have responded to such a situation, although it seemed as if his reticence had been pushed aside for something he had lacked but hoped for all of his life—the possibility of a genuine relationship.

Bob went on to describe how they exchanged phone numbers and then finally got together three days later. He told me about the anticipation and nervousness he felt during those three days—how he had obsessed about Ken and counted the moments until he would see him once again.

"I tried to recall," said Bob, "exactly what he looked like. Were his eyes blue or gray? Was he as good looking as I remembered? Would he be as nice to me in a restaurant as he was in the bookstore? Would we have enough to talk about?"

It was obvious that Bob had been smitten by Ken's attractiveness.

"When I saw him sitting in the corner booth, my heart jumped," said Bob. "He was even more wonderful than I had remembered, and we spent three hours there in that restaurant, just talking and falling in love."

It was at this point that tears abruptly appeared in Bob's eyes and he couldn't continue. Bob was choking with emotion. I felt moved to step to his side and put my arms around him. He hugged me hard as the tears spilled all over both of us. It felt as if he never wanted to let go. He cried like this in my arms for a good ten minutes.

"It's all my fault," he stammered as he searched his pockets for a handkerchief.

"What's all your fault?" I asked gently.

"Ken's dead," he said, "and it's all my fault." Bob began to shake all over, uncontrollably. I wanted to hold on even tighter, as if I could calm the tremors in his body.

It took about half an hour under these circumstances to at last uncover the source of Bob's trauma. It was a poignant description of a relationship that had begun in a bigger-than-life, rhapsodic kind of way, and had ended tragically and prematurely.

"We were in the park," said Bob. "Well, where else could we go? There's sure no place out in public where we could go and hold hands and be ourselves."

He was right. "Such a simple thing," I thought. "Holding hands—looking at your lover in a special way—being giddy and silly together—why should it be so hard?"

"We were in that part of Schenley Park known as the 'Fruit Loop,'" said Bob, eyes blurred and red. The memories of this must have been horrible. He was certain of every detail as he told about the configuration of trees and buildings and cars.

I wondered how people like Bob must feel having to go to a place called the "Fruit Loop" in order to enjoy those simple things that the average straight couple can take for granted in any public place.

"We had just gotten out of the car and were walking across the grass," he said.

Bob could hardly speak, he was so tormented with the intensity of the memories and feelings. "I wanted to sit on the hillside and watch the sunset with Ken, but I forgot to bring the blanket, so I asked him if he would mind going back to the car after it." Bob's voice dropped to almost a whisper. "Oh God, why did I ever meet him? Why did I ever suggest that we go to the park that night? It's all my fault," he cried. "Ken could still be alive if it weren't for me! I'll never forgive myself!"

I sat numbed as Bob told me what had happened. Apparently the "Fruit Loop" is a place known by others besides the gay men who go there. It has become a kind of joke and a dare for certain people—mostly men—who get a kick out of having a few drinks, and then, just for laughs, go to the park to harass any "fags" they might find there. This is what was going on that night. One of the cars parked in the shadows along the curb held four men who were pumped up on beer just waiting for some unsuspecting "queers" to show up. By the time Bob and Ken got there the men were itching to cause trouble.

In the few moments that it took Ken to retrieve the blanket, turn around, and head back to where Bob was, the bullies had piled out of their car and were waiting for him, unnoticed.

Evidently, the most brazen of the four hurled an empty bottle at Ken, who fell to the ground. Bob wasn't too clear on this part because he didn't see what happened—he had been looking the other way. But it must have hit Ken in the back of the head because he had a deep cut there. It wasn't until the men started yelling and jeering at Ken, who appeared to be unconscious, that Bob turned and saw the horror of what was going on.

The men were kicking Ken in the back and chest. They were bellowing slurred obscenities at him—calling him a "f---ing queer." "How do ya like that, SWEEEETIE!" they hooted. "Doesn't that feel good you f---ing bastard!"

By then, Bob had run to Ken's side and was trying desperately to grab his arms and drag him away. Bob was clearly not a fighter. The best he could do was to take a couple of swings at the ones who were doing most of the kicking and then throw himself on top of Ken's bruised and bleeding body, where he also got kicked and slammed by fists and feet. He was frantic. By then, blood was everywhere. He was terrified for both of their lives.

"Hey, girlfriend," they taunted. "Bet you like THIS, don't you?" One of the men was yanking at Bob's pants, trying to tear them off, while another was holding onto his ankles. Bob said he started yelling as loudly as he could for help and one of the brutes, a brawny, curly-haired, weight-lifter type, slugged him so hard in the face that it knocked him out. That's the last thing he remembers before he came to and saw Ken's dead body next to him in the grass beside the blood-stained blanket.

Bob's grief was inconsolable at that moment. All I could do was to continue to hold him as we rocked back and forth and cried. My own anguish virtually paralyzed me as I thought about the senselessness of Ken's death. Those men weren't out there to steal money or to pay back an evil deed. There was no singular reason for this outrageous attack and murder except that Ken and Bob were gay, and they happened to be in the wrong place at the wrong time. The drunkards had gone there to have a little "fun" and they let it go too far. No one had heard the screams. No one came to help. No one has yet found the murderers, because there were no witnesses, other than Bob, and the police had very little information to use in their investigation.

Bob is haunted by this nightmare night and day. There is no convincing him that this atrocious act was not his fault. It occurred to me that Bob might never risk a relationship again. He had just discovered he was gay. He had met his first true love. He had managed to open up enough to let himself experience how gratifying and life-giving and rich a relationship can be. And this was how it turned out. Such a setback—not only in relationship, but in coming out—could prove to be insurmountable.

I doubt that Bob's pain will ever go away. How could it? Yet he has reached out to begin the healing process, and that, at least, is a beginning. I never saw Bob again after the day he shared this story with me. I often wonder how he is doing. And on those occasions when I happen to be in the vicinity of the Fruit Loop, I think about him.

## Charlene

*Looking for love in all the wrong places, until...*

Coming out stories are unique—some tragic, some surprising, some amusing. For Charlene, it was a long and complicated process, but now that she knows she is a lesbian, she is able to joke about the circumstances along the way that were humorous, and she has developed a certain lightheartedness that serves her well.

I ran into Charlene at a party. She was the center of attention, holding a drink in her hand, surrounded by other women who were all laughing and chatting together. Charlene is fun to be with, and I guessed that, since this was a "gay" party, these women were possibly lesbians who were flirting with Charlene because she is so easygoing, attractive, and upbeat. I joined the conversation for a while, and eventually the other women moved off to join another cluster of women on the patio, giving me a chance to become acquainted with this very likeable person.

Charlene and I were comparing children and the challenges of motherhood, finding that we had some things in common. As we talked, we discovered that we also shared the identity of being divorced women. I was curious about that. When did she realize that she was a lesbian? Before or after the divorce?

"To tell you the truth, Renee," she explained as she downed the last of her drink, "I've been married and divorced THREE times!" Charlene's eyes opened wide with expression as she held up three fingers to emphasize. "Do you believe it?" She seemed to think this was so farfetched that she was shaking her head in amazement. "Three times—then I finally figured it out."

"How did that happen," I asked.

"Well," she said, "I married the first time because I was young and just out of high school, and all my friends were getting married and I thought that's what I wanted—I didn't know much about love, but I liked this guy and he loved me, so we got married. He's the father of my two kids."

So far, Charlene's story was similar to my own.

"After fifteen years I realized I didn't love my husband—that I never had loved him and besides that, we hadn't had sex in about five years. So he was starting to run around, and I didn't care because I knew I didn't want to have sex with him. The idea of it would really turn me off. I figured our marriage was probably never meant to be—the fact that I didn't care about the other women told me something too. So we split up and I met this guy named Rob. I now recognize the fact that I married him on the rebound, and I'm embarrassed that I didn't see it at the time. He said things I really wanted to hear, but there wasn't much depth to our relationship. It turns out, I should've gotten to know him a lot more than I did, because he was a liar and I didn't know it until it was too late."

Charlene stopped to slide an ice cube into her mouth and crack it to pieces with her teeth. "Well, that wouldn't have made any difference anyway, as it turns out," she said indifferently. "I didn't know then what I know now. After I divorced Rob I did wait to find 'Mr. Right.' This man was really attractive and stable and honest—and rich. I decided by that time, 'why not find somebody who's rich?' So after dating him for two years we got married. I don't know what I thought happiness was supposed to be, but I found out it didn't have much to do with being rich."

So far, Charlene hadn't said anything that I hadn't heard before from some of my straight friends. Then the story changed.

"It was about a year into my third marriage when I confessed to myself that I wasn't happy. But I couldn't figure out why. I had everything that money could buy. I was married to a man who paid a lot of attention to me, but for some reason, I wasn't able to return his affection in the way that he wanted. In other words, I saw that sex just wasn't important to me—in fact, it had never really been important to me. I could easily do without it, and each husband I had would have problems with me around this. We would usually end up having big fights about it and we'd both end up feeling rejected somehow."

"That's too bad," I said, "did you ever try counseling?"

"Oh," Charlene laughed. "I hate to tell you the amount of money I've spent on counseling." She popped another ice cube into her mouth.

I was really curious by then. "So when did you...well...how did you..."

"Discover I'm a lesbian?" she asked between crunches.

"Yes," I replied, feeling a bit awkward.

Charlene shrugged casually. "When I fell head over heels in love with a woman," she said grinning, as she slid the last piece of ice into her mouth.

"Oh," I said, and managed a smile.

"I never dreamed it would happen to me," said Charlene. "It caught me totally off guard. I met this woman in a class I was taking and—shazam! It was all over. I never knew it could happen like that. And it turned out, she was a lesbian who kinda liked me, too."

"That's amazing," I said.

"Well, what's amazing is that when I met her and got to know her, I realized that I was in love for the first time in my life. I mean REALLY in love! Now that I can look back on my marriages, it makes perfect sense that they never worked out. How could they have? There was this one huge important piece missing from the puzzle. And now that I know what it is, I can say, 'Of course.' That's what it was all that time. Thank God I finally figured it out."

Charlene finished her sentence with an air of triumph as she lifted her empty glass above her head and beamed. No, it had not been painless for her or the men she had married. No, it did not make sense to her children or family, caught in the wake of relational tragedy. No, she did not immediately find a long-term, intimate relationship where she could live happily ever after. But for the first time in her life, Charlene knew what she was all about, and she knew what she wanted—and what she didn't want.

This was, relatively speaking, an ordinary conversation between two women, a pastor and laywoman, about marriage and divorce, love and brokenness. As everyday as this matter sounds, Charlene's story would be unwelcome and impossible to share in most churches. Whereas there are many places in the secular world where sexual minorities like Charlene can now talk about these things, it is disappointing that the church is the very place where certain deep personal struggles are met with rejection, judgment, and hostility. This happens because blind adherence to tradition keeps Christians from being able to really hear and understand the pain from personal experience that falls outside of Christian acceptability.

We need to make the church a place where the sexual minority community can come to draw upon our spiritual resources: hospitality, compassion, love; where people in pain, no matter who they are, no matter what their struggle, can find a home that is nurturing, embracing, and life-giving. That seems to be the appropriate identity for the Christian church, but we are not there yet.

## CHAPTER 7

# Special Couples:
# Kathy and Claire, Stewart and Tim, and Russell and Carl

*"The deepest need of humankind is the need to overcome separateness, to leave the prison of aloneness." —Erich Fromm*

We have seen glimpses of how gay men and lesbians experience the phenomenon of falling in love with the same feelings, energy, and intensity as heterosexuals. Once coupled, however, the same-sex pairs often encounter some unique problems that are not present for couples with heterosexual privilege. The next three stories describe this kind of difference. The challenges of living in a same-sex relationship certainly present all of the issues involved in heterosexual ones, but much more. Can the church be more than welcoming to these couples? Can it be affirming as well?

## Kathy and Claire
*All they wanted was a public validation of their union...*

Kathy and Claire are a couple in their fifties who have been together for two and a half years. Kathy had been married to a man at one time in her life, although she didn't have any children from her marriage, and discovered only about five years ago that she was a lesbian. She met Claire about a year after Claire had ended her second important lesbian relationship. They were ready to meet one another—the timing was right because each understood what the other had been through. It was a worthy bond, strengthened by their common experience and the delightful match that they had found in each other.

They both enjoyed similar hobbies and interests. They shared like values and goals. They were deeply in love. Neither one had ever committed herself to someone in a more profound, meaningful, long-term way. They couldn't imagine living without being together, and they wanted their relationship blessed and witnessed by their friends and families in a holy union ceremony.

Claire and Kathy shared with me the difficulties they had in planning their celebration. This type of event is much more problematic than a wedding planned by a straight couple. To begin with, they couldn't be sure that any of the service providers they contacted would deal honestly with them, because of homophobia or malicious mischief toward gays, or fear that if the straight community found out the store served such couples they would lose straight business. For example, when they went to a tuxedo rental service to rent two matching tuxedos for themselves, how could they be certain that the shop would give them proper sizes, clean apparel, and timely delivery? How could they be absolutely sure that the caterer would treat them with respect and use the same fresh ingredients that straight couples would get? What if the baker, florist, DJ, or photographer sabotaged them somehow? Where would they find a hall for the reception? All of these concerns were foremost on the minds of Kathy and Claire as they made arrangements for their special day.

It became more and more stressful as they were required to speak with strangers over the telephone and explain the situation, waiting for the reaction on the other end of the line. Some folks were friendly and helpful, others were rude and obnoxious. And what could the two women do about this? Call the Better Business Bureau? Where could they find what they needed, and what recourse did they have if, on account of their sexual orientation, they were ill-treated? The whole process was a challenge and a real test of their relationship—certainly more so than a straight couple in the same situation.

Difficulties with the business world were only half the battle for Kathy and Claire. They also had to face up to the feelings of various family members and friends regarding an invitation to such an event. In almost every case, the persons they were going to invite to the union had never been to such an occasion. It was a new level of coming out. Previously, Kathy and Claire had arrived together at parties and family gatherings, and their identity as a couple was not discussed because it was easier for the others to deny it than to talk openly about it. Now that there was to be a holy union—now that there would be formal invitations with the specific words embossed on elegant paper—how could ambivalent family members and friends continue to be in denial? The question kept coming up as to whether it would be better just not to invite certain people, or to use the occasion as a way of teaching or raising consciousness about long-term, committed gay relationships. In either case, their frustration about having to make such judgments is moot for most average straight couples.

Kathy's parents really liked Claire, so they were not going to cause a problem, but Claire's father, who is her only living parent, was not so accommodating. He refused to come, as did Claire's younger sister. Other siblings, nieces, and cousins divided rather evenly between pro and con, but the two women decided to send all of them invitations anyway. At the workplace, Kathy had some friends who knew she was a lesbian and would be happy to receive an invitation. Others, to whom Kathy was not out, were friends whom she wanted to invite, but she was afraid she might alienate them. At Claire's office those who work closely with her knew that she was lesbian, but other important colleagues, such as her boss and secretary, did not. They would wonder why everyone else was chatting about getting invitations, when they had not received one.

All in all, it seemed that some of the dynamics present in preparing a guest list for a straight wedding were likewise part of this situation; the big difference was that, in addition to the puzzle of who gets invited, there was also the circumstance whereby the invitees (and others who heard about the event but were not invited) would learn that the two persons extending such an announcement were gay.

In spite of all this, Claire and Kathy's holy union ceremony went well. They had done the necessary research to find gay-friendly professionals so they could trust the quality of what they received, and that process had taken its toll in added stress and aggravation as details were worked through. But they were glad they had such an event. It was a message to their loved ones that they wanted to be recognized, as any other couple would be, as having a sacred bond—not just a secular one.

Of course, a holy union service is not a legal ceremony; there are no papers filed with the state; the two are not recognized as spousal partners in matters of health insurance and similar things. Yet these two women hoped, by virtue of this public rite, to establish an understanding with their families around some of these legalities. For example, they hoped that family members would honor the wish that the beneficiary on each of their life insurance policies would be her partner. They hope their families will understand, if not accept, that the two women have adjusted their last will and testament and living will papers to reflect the new status of their relationship.

For many similar reasons, the holy union of Kathy and Claire, blessed by a celebrant and witnessed by others, was of great spiritual significance. The company that gathered to participate in that holy union celebration would hopefully view the relationship of Claire and Kathy in a new, more reverent way, from that moment on. And they will all have grown because of it. Normally, an event of such spiritual and relational significance is done in the context of church life and community. Kathy and Claire and countless couples like them will plan, provide, and participate in these celebrations without the knowledge or consent of a congregation that could be surrounding them with love and support in their life's journey together. Can the church be both welcoming and affirming for them?

## Stewart and Tim

*Their relationship was wonderful, but they wanted something more—something their straight friends enjoyed...*

Another couple, Stewart and Tim, never had a holy union ceremony, but they have been together in an exclusive, committed, and loving relationship for almost twenty years. Stewart wanted to talk with me one day; he had an exciting idea and wanted to know what I would think about it. He and Tim have found their companionship with one another deeply satisfying after all those years, yet they felt that something was missing, something that would validate even more the closeness and caring that they had for each other. They wanted eagerly to have a baby.

As Stewart shared this dream with me, he held his breath and studied my face to see how I would react. I was thrilled. Everything I knew about the two men told me that they would be excellent parents. They are both kind and gracious, loving and patient.

"Stewart," I said, reaching for his hands. "I think that's a wonderful idea."

Stewart exhaled with resonant laughter. I could see that the prospect of his being a father was one that touched Stewart's warmest, most nurturing side. After a few moments of light-hearted conversation about the marvels of babies and parenthood, I raised the obvious question, "How will you do this?" (Stewart suddenly couldn't resist joking about what he might look like pregnant.)

Then he said, "I'm not sure, but Tim and I have tried to look at all the options."

My mind raced with possibilities. I had read a lot of articles about gay couples as parents, and I knew that he and Tim might consider several avenues. Had they thought about finding a surrogate mother, a female friend or relative who would agree to provide an ovum for in vitro fertilization and carry the child? Tim and Stewart would only have to decide which one of them would provide the sperm.

"We've thought of that," he said. "Tim has a sister, but he and Mandy don't have a close enough relationship to ask such a monumental favor. Our best female friends are married and we don't feel right about asking one of them to disrupt their entire life for this. There's no one in my family I could ask."

"What a shame," I thought, "that these two men can't have the joys and privileges of parenthood simply because they are gay. Surely there must be a way."

"The way that makes the most sense to us," he continued, "is to apply to an adoption agency. It will take some time and effort—and expense—but it will be worth it if we can find a baby. We have the names of a few agencies that might help us."

I wondered how, when a gay couple has as much trouble as Claire and Kathy did planning a holy union, two gay men would find an adoption agency that would cooperate with them in finding a healthy baby to adopt. This seemed like so much more an insurmountable task. Yet Stewart was hopeful and enthusiastic and asked me if I would write a reference for them if things progressed that far.

"Of course I will," I said. "I'll say only wonderful things about you and Tim."

Stewart left my office that day filled with happy dreams about babies and parenthood and forming a new family. Some little child would be fortunate, indeed, I mused, to have Tim and Stewart as its parents. I prayed that I might see the day.

Within two years, it happened. Stewart came to church one Sunday morning with the jubilant news that he and Tim would soon have a one-month-old baby girl. He had given me progress reports from time to time, but they had often involved setbacks and false promises, so when this breakthrough occurred, Stewart could barely contain himself. He looked as if he was about to burst with excitement. And I rejoiced with him.

How did this happen? They had found an agency that would agree to a single parent adoption, and Stewart was the formal applicant. The references and home visits were excellent, and the agency found no reason not to let Stewart adopt this beautiful child. When all the paperwork was finalized, baby Carolyn was brought before the congregation by "Daddy" Stewart and "Papa" Tim for the sacrament of holy baptism. Several of Tim and Stewart's family had flown in from out of town to witness this most meaningful event along with other friends, and when they gathered around the baptism font many folks were crying with Stewart and Tim as we shared that memorable day.

Claire and Kathy and Stewart and Tim are very lucky, as couples, to have supportive communities around them where they can share their joys and sorrows. Not all gay couples are as blessed, as I learned from persons such as Russell, when he told me about his spousal relationship with Carl.

## Russell and Carl

*The greatest joy in life became the source of the greatest pain...*

It was Russell who most helped me to see how the world assumes that people are, or used to be, or should be, part of a male-female couple, if they are to be coupled at all. This assumption is central to how we are acculturated, yet it is so subtle that it goes unnoticed. For example, when people go to an event where name tags are worn, traditionally-named heterosexual couples (ones who share the same last name) can be easily identified as married. Their name tags reflect it, as do wedding rings, if they are wearing them. It is not uncommon at social events to introduce one's significant other and to touch each other affectionately, hold hands, or show couple identity in some other visible way.

With gay couples at straight social functions, however, none of this is usually true. If two closeted gay men go to a party together, they are most likely perceived and introduced as roommates. They would not be wearing recognized wedding rings. They would not steal a kiss from the other or hold hands, and, possibly, they would mingle with people in different parts of the room, to lessen suspicion that they belong together. Their conversation would probably be kept to safe topics regarding their partner, and most people would have no awareness of the tremendous amount of information and emotion that must be suppressed, in contrast to what is acceptable and allowed for straight couples. Add to this the fact that single women at the party may find the men attractive and flirt with them, and you have a formula for a kind of genteel schizophrenia.

Russell worked in the sort of place where, if it became known that he was gay and living with a life partner, he would be fired immediately and unconditionally. I could imagine how cruel office parties were for Russell, in that he was never able to bring Carl with him. In fact, people at the office didn't even know Carl existed. It was a tightrope that Russell had to walk every time he was asked questions about his personal life, his vacations, his holidays, his love life. There was virtually nothing that Russell could share about any of this, and, to make matters worse, people at work were always trying to fix him up with women they knew. Russell became an expert at withholding information because he didn't especially like having to lie outright, although he was forced to do that sometimes.

Russell and Carl were together for seventeen years when Carl developed a deadly form of leukemia that dragged on for months. At one level there were difficulties with some of the hospital medical staff who were prejudiced against gays. Russell would try to be there as much as possible in the evenings and on weekends during those critical times, and he got to know who the "friendly" hospital staff were and those who were hostile or rude.

Not all of Carl's family members were gracious to Russell when they would come to visit the hospital. They wanted to be the ones to make decisions and talk with the doctors and other caretakers. Some of them were mean to Russell and treated him with contempt, accusing him of being insensitive for staying there when the family wanted to be in the room. They were the same way when it came to making funeral plans. Most family members completely ignored Russell's suggestions, in spite of the fact that he was trying to convey wishes that Carl had specifically spelled out when he had been well enough to talk about things.

The hospital stays were, physically and emotionally, always a big drain on Russell, but that was only the half of it. During those times, Russell's work suffered. He was exhausted most of the time and more prone to be depressed and make mistakes, in addition to not being able to share with anyone at the office what was really going on. When Russell needed to take a personal day to put Carl in the hospice, no one knew what the problem was. It was as if Russell was living two lives.

When Carl finally died, Russell had gone almost three days without sleep, wanting to be with his true love in those final moments. He felt it was the ultimate gift that he was alone with Carl, holding his hand at his final breath. He was the one who then contacted Carl's family. The funeral was dreadful because it seemed to Russell that Carl's parents did everything their own way and left him out of all the major decisions. Worse, he had not been included in some things (such as the pre- and post-visitation viewings), which involved only the immediate family.

All things considered, this was the most devastating experience of loss in Russell's entire life and not one person at work even knew about it. He had had to use his vacation days for the three weeks during and after the funeral, when he was so torn apart he could hardly move, and through it all there was not a sympathy card or a supportive word or a measure of understanding from anyone from the office. Moreover, he was expected to come and go from his job as if nothing had happened.

When a wife or husband dies, the office sends flowers, food, and other tokens, the bereaved partner is often given some measure of slack because of the stress and depression of such a loss, and colleagues show support by coming to the funeral home for visitation or services. However, in Russell's case, and for countless others like him, no mention is ever made of the true reason for the time off and the sadness. Russell was expected to do his work and resume leadership responsibilities and presentations as if every day were just as ordinary as the next. One wonders how long such couples will have to wait before they are afforded the same privileges that straights enjoy.

It is this sort of pretense about sexual identity in the workplace and other settings that creates fear, denial, and hurt in our churches as well. It is time for the church to support non-heterosexuals by developing rituals for holy unions; to encourage gay, lesbian, and bisexual couples to have and raise children, and to welcome them at the baptismal font; to minister to non-heterosexual couples in other ways as they move through the joys and struggles of their common lives together. But it must be intentional. As long as the church believes that the practice of homosexuality is a sin, we will not be open to any of this. We will close the door to wholesome, loving, and faithful same-sex coupling. At the same time, a narrow Christian perspective that disallows healthy same-sex coupling actually helps to encourage what the church most condemns: multiple relationships and promiscuity. When will we open our eyes and see the connection, allowing experiences, such as those of the same-sex couples here, to move us toward Christian teaching that addresses the real issues in their lives?

CHAPTER 8

# People In the Middle:
# José, Betty, and Dawn

*"Be kind. Remember, everyone you meet*
*is fighting a hard battle."*
—*T. H. Thompson*

The stories I share represent more than just those of homosexuals. To be limited to that identity alone is to leave out a lot of other people. When I first became aware of the so-called "gay community," I thought about it in terms of that one "other" group—namely, homosexuals. It seemed to me that the basic issues had to do with "straights" versus "gays", and how a person from one group would relate to a person from the other group. Homosexuality had become an emotionally charged topic in the church across denominational lines, and almost the entire debate around it and the subsequent study documents had to do with homosexuality: whether it is a sin; how it is caused; how to relate to gay people in the church. It wasn't until after I was working in this area for some years that I saw how utterly confining this distinction is for persons who are neither gay nor straight. To further complicate the spectrum, there are transgendered persons in various states of being: pre-op (those waiting for gender-corrective surgery), post-op (those who have already had the surgery), and non-op (those who are not planning to have surgery, but who have made the outward adjustments). And after gender-corrective adjustments have been made (with or without surgery), the persons still have an orientational identity that is gay, lesbian, or bisexual. Having said all this may help you to see that dividing the world into two groups—straights and gays—is as absurd as trying to describe a rainbow using only two colors.

The concept of a spectrum of diversity is a struggle for many straight people (as well as gay), who do not relate as well to bisexuals, transsexuals, transvestites, and others who are not self-identified exclusively as gay or straight. Much progress has been made because of pride events, to recognize, appreciate, and include all persons within the scope of the "gay" community, but we all have a long way to go on this.

The next three persons are among the most invisible to the church because we in the church have confined our attention to such a small part of the gender minority community. Others remain somewhere in oblivion in relation to the life of the church. Bisexuals are also in our congregations, but we don't know it, based on appearances. They look like anyone else. Transgendered people tend to stay away from church because differences in appearance may stand out as noticeable or offensive, and this would prove to be the ultimate test of learning to love *everyone*, including the furthest outcast. Perhaps if the church were to move at least to a place of recognition and issue the challenge to love and accept these children of God, they would risk making their presence known.

## José

*He loves men and women equally, so neither gays nor straights want to claim him...*

José is a bisexual man. His friendship is a very special gift to me, because he is helping me to understand that sexual identity and attraction are not as simple as most people think. Because bisexuality is not easily accepted and understood, by straight society or even other orientations, José has been grappling with his sexuality for many years. Bisexuals are not fully affirmed by straights or gays. Finding support and information is an ongoing problem for José.

A bisexual person is a man or woman who is equally attracted to males and females. Even this definition is woefully lacking, because there are several considerations that have an impact on any designation of sexual identity, such as what gender someone fantasizes about, loves, or behaves sexually toward, at various levels. Does this person always have a same-gendered love or fantasy object? Does this vary according to certain circumstances, and what would those circumstances be? Beyond that, is this person just now self-identifying in this way, or is this a past indication, or perhaps a desired ideal? As people such as José discover, it becomes extremely complicated to state simply and definitely once and for all one's sexual orientation.

José has come to accept his bisexuality, but not without a lot of turmoil and alienation. After he accepted it, he had to make some big decisions as to what he would do about it. First of all, he told me what it was like to sort through relationships when looking for commitment. As he talked about this process, I recognized that all of us, in searching for intimacy, must prioritize our relationships. For example, if I, as a straight single person, go to a party with the intention of meeting a man, my eyes scan the crowd for men whom I find attractive. If my focus were to find a prospective relationship, I might place myself in a setting where I have an opportunity to engage one of these men in a conversation, during which time I will probably discover if this man is married or not, if he is already coupled, and various other bits of data about his life, work, and so forth. If I find he is married, or sexist, or a bigot, or anything else that is inconsistent with my values, I would eventually move on to talk with someone else. Chances are, I will spend less time engaging the women in conversation, unless they are grouped with the attractive men I would want to meet.

Over the course of the evening I will have prioritized the guests at the party and applied certain criteria—all of which is not really a conscious process for most people, especially at an average party, and even less likely in everyday places such as the workplace, campus, or supermarket. It happens in so subtle a way that we may not realize it is going on, unless we are really deliberate and everyone at the event has a similar agenda, such as a singles' get-acquainted party. Yet it happens.

The reason I elaborate on this is to make it easier to understand what happens when someone like José, a bisexual person, finds himself in similar situations. Certainly, he will use his own filters when prioritizing the relationships at the party, such as attractiveness, availability, values, etc. But José is not limited to pursuing a relationship with only the women in the room. His prioritization process, conscious or not, encompasses many more people than mine, by virtue of the fact that he is able to relate with men and women with equal interest. If he goes to that same party wanting to meet someone, his starting place may already include almost every person in the room.

Along with the added difficulties for bisexuals such as José to identify a partner, there are negative and disapproving attitudes from both the gay and straight communities toward bisexuals. Straight persons use the same judgments and rationales to condemn bisexuals as they do for gay people, and tend to lump them together. Because bisexuals have an aspect of same-sex attraction, they are not fully accepted by the straight world. The same is true about attitudes coming from gay people. Because bisexuals can couple with opposite-sex partners, gays accuse them of "copping out" of the struggles of being a sexual minority by taking the easy route: choosing the straight option. These negative attitudes from all sides add complications to many facets of the bisexual's life, including how to make social and moral choices about coupling. Here again, the church is not equipped to counsel bisexuals in a relevant way, as long as we have a moral code that applies only to heterosexuals and that sees coupling with an eye toward procreation.

To describe this in terms of Jose's experience, he admitted it was like being in a quagmire much of the time. The complexities boggled my mind. I realized how grateful I was to not be a bisexual person. How much easier my life seemed all of a sudden.

After having experienced the strain of this predicament for much of his adult life and having had relationships with various men and women, Jose was ready to make a life-changing decision. He had fallen in love with a straight woman, had dated her for two years, and wrestled the whole time with what to do with the other half of his identity. She loved him back, and they had discussed marriage many times. In order to be honest and open with her, José confessed that he was bisexual. To her credit, Carol did not reject him for this reason. She loved him too much.

José and Carol married. This decision was celebrated by family, friends, and fellows churchgoers. But José's secret journey, which was much more complicated than I could imagine, added a rich poignancy to his resolve to choose Carol over all the others.

As I think about José and other bisexual people, I wonder if the task for them would be any easier if the church would be a place for guidance and counsel beyond the traditional mandate of heterosexual marriage. Could the church be a place to promote acceptance of bisexuals within different communities? In addition, suppose that José had chosen a man to be his life partner? It is difficult to imagine that most fellow churchgoers would celebrate that decision, even though it would represent an equal commitment to monogamy. José's experience helps me to see the inadequacy of church teachings in a unique way.

## Betty
*She wants her difference to be accepted, but it shows...*

If José would have trouble getting relevant guidance and support from the church, think for a moment about other people in the middle—from the even more isolated transgendered community.

Meet Betty. Betty feels like a new person, because in many ways, she is. I first saw her at a social gathering where she was standing across the room at the refreshment table holding a little plate filled with assorted cheese squares, fruit pieces, and crackers. She seemed very alone, even though lots of people would gravitate to the table where she was standing. Yet after brief interchanges, Betty would be standing there without company again. I noticed this and decided to go over to meet her.

I introduced myself and she smiled broadly, holding out her free hand to shake mine—a hand that was very large, as was the rest of her frame, noticeable especially in her shoulders, thighs and feet. Her name tag said simply "Betty," and up close I could see that she was wearing an ash blonde wig and several layers of foundation under her makeup, which, along with precisely defined red-orange lips and dangling rhinestone earrings, gave her an unusual appearance. She had a cleft chin and rugged features, except for the long black eyelashes that were pressed to her lids, just below the line of purple shadow. Her beige dress was comely and hugged her waist and hips before it flared slightly to below the knee. Betty's high-heeled shoes on such large feet were conspicuous, but tastefully coordinated with her other apparel.

"Nice to meet you," she said in a low, resonant voice. I have to admit, I was taken aback in the face of her "differentness." But then, remembering the reason I came over to meet this person, I resolved to ride out my feelings of awkwardness in order to get to know her.

I struck up a conversation about the occasion that brought us together and tried to lightheartedly steer it to a topic where Betty might feel free to share her story with me. She seemed to relax a bit as we talked and I also found myself loosening up a bit with the chatter. We even managed to attract a couple more people to our little repartee, and it seemed that Betty was enjoying herself.

As we stood and talked together I tried to imagine what it would be like to be Betty. She had obviously spent a great deal of time carefully applying makeup, styling her wig, selecting her dress, shoes, and accessories, and she wanted to feel welcomed and valued. She was not an exhibitionist; in fact, she was rather shy, and was trying hard to make friends at this party, even though many people seemed to feel uneasy around her.

I watched her as she interacted with the others. She was reaching out in her own congenial way to be sociable. She wanted to be as attractive as she could be. She had made choices that would affect how others felt about her and perceived her as a person. These must have been difficult choices—but then, maybe they were not really choices at all. Maybe she had struggled with the easy way and realized that the easy way was not the honest way for her—that for her, to be really true to herself, she would risk social alienation and discomfort in order to claim her true personhood and identity. This was, perhaps, something that was beyond choice; it was the only way to be at home with who she is and wants most to be.

As I thought about what Betty must go through each and every time she encounters a stranger at the store or on the street or at a party, I found that I admired her profoundly for her courage to be true to who she really is. I could do no less and no more. Most of us work hard into adulthood sorting out all these issues, but for persons such as Betty, societal expectations and implications vastly compound and complicate even the ordinary developmental tasks of life. Betty helped me to appreciate this work even more, especially as I thought about her spiritual needs and whether the church helped or did not help to meet them.

## Dawn

*Her way of being was natural to her, but repulsive to some...*

Dawn is a person who put my newfound appreciation to the test more than anyone else. She, like Betty, was one who unwittingly attracted attention because of her unexpected persona. Dawn had no fashion sense. She dressed in a way that reminded me of some of my younger friends who often go "thrifting" (purchasing clothes at thrift stores), but Dawn's way of combining polyester and broadcloth was dowdy at best, certainly without flair or creativity. From under pleated, flowery skirts and sleeve hems of silky blouses with neck bows and rhinestone buttons could be seen big, beefy legs and arms, neatly shaved. Her purses, sweaters, and belts were similar to ones from the thirties that my grandmother wore.

Dawn's voice was smooth but strained as she maintained a pitch above a point where the ordinary voice would break from normal sound levels into falsetto. When I heard her speak I would feel my own throat tighten as I wanted to swallow for her, as if relaxing the vocal chords would soften the sonority of the sound back to a depth that seemed more appropriate to the size of the person speaking. Nonetheless, her manner as she talked was always pleasant, and she seemed eager for friendship and conversation.

Dawn's facial hair had been carefully plucked in most places, except on the skin under her chin, where an abundance of stubble suggested that there was too much growth to pluck and shaving had had its consequences. She wore a black shoulder length wig and seemed to have a large variety of costume rings—the big, sparkly kind with lots of stones and facets—which she wore on several fingers at once to accent her long, polished nails. Whenever I saw Dawn, I was endeared to her by the statement she chose to make in the way she presented herself, without apology, to everyone she met. She wasn't presumptuous; in fact, her vulnerability was refreshing. Somehow she had found her "way" in the world. In an odd sort of manner, it worked, and I liked her.

One day I received a phone call from Dawn. Her voice was very faint and weak on the other end of the line, and it was difficult to hear what she was saying. She was telling me that she had just been admitted to the hospital for some major emergency surgery for an aneurysm somewhere in her chest, and she wanted me to know it so that I could pray for her. After describing the situation to me, she started to choke up with emotion, and the already strained voice cracked a couple of times. I immediately prayed with her on the telephone and then promised to be with her at the hospital when she came out of the recovery room, assuming she lived through the dangers of the operation.

Dawn was tremendously relieved and grateful to see me there. She had obviously been terrified of the surgical procedure that had been performed on her and was also in a great deal of pain. The hospital staff had removed her wig, but she was wearing a blue scrub hat, which hugged her head about the ears and puffed out against the pillow behind the oxygen tubes that ran up to the silver regulator on the wall behind her bed. I only stayed a few minutes that first visit because Dawn was exhausted and a bit delirious from the anesthetic. However, the next time I went to see her, she was able to talk to me.

"Renee," she whispered with a smile as she saw me enter the room. "I'm so glad to see you." Dawn was still hooked up to several lines and contraptions with beeping noises and computerized numbers and lights. "This intensive care unit is a madhouse." She reached out her hand so I could hold it.

"How are things going?" I asked.

"All I know is, I'm alive," she said weakly. "I hope to go to a regular room tomorrow."

That was good news, based on the ordeal that Dawn had just been through. It must have meant that she was making good progress.

"I'm glad," I said as I squeezed her hand gently. "I'll look for you there next time I come in."

I prayed with Dawn and then turned to leave. As I stepped to the door she hollered at me with a louder whisper. "Oh, Renee."

I hurried back to her bedside.

"Will you bring me communion next time you come? I asked the chaplain—the one here in the hospital—to bring me the eucharist when I was admitted to the hospital, but he never came back. I don't know why. Would you do that for me?"

"Of course," I answered.

When I returned the next time, I brought my communion box with me. There are times when I know that the recipient really appreciates this gesture as a healing rite of the church, but in this case with Dawn, the depth of gratitude was especially noticeable and profound, as she thanked me again and again. I spent some time chatting with Dawn about her future: what the doctors had to say about her condition, what dietary considerations she might have, what medications she would have to be on for the rest of her life. Overall, she was upbeat because her life had been in grave danger and just being alive was a victory.

As I prepared to leave, I drew nearer to Dawn's face to pray, held her hand in mine, while my other hand rested on her shoulder. I closed my eyes and prayed aloud with words of thanksgiving for the success of the surgery and the progress Dawn was making. While doing this, I heard rushed footsteps that had come from down the hall enter Dawn's room and stop suddenly, apparently in reverence to the fact that I was in the midst of a prayer. Someone was breathing rapidly in the doorway, and I could hear the sound of paperwork being shuffled from hand to hand. I finished my prayer and looked up to see a nurse waiting patiently for me to conclude my business with Dawn so she could proceed with hers.

This ordinary moment, which happens again and again in the course of hospital visitation, became one of the most extraordinarily memorable and poignant times that I will ever know as a Christian minister. Why? Because the nurse had come into Dawn's room with something in her hand that, again, was perfectly commonplace, yet made a world of difference in the way that I would perceive Dawn in that moment and for the rest of my friendship with her. The nurse stepped up to the bed, and attached an apparatus to the railing that literally divided the space between Dawn and me by mere inches. It was a male urinal.

I was looking into Dawn's eyes at the exact time that the nurse hooked the handle of the urinal in place, brushing it against my arm in the process. One of my hands was still holding her hand; my other hand still resting lightly upon her shoulder. This was one of those exaggerated, slow motion, freeze-frame times of life when I was keenly aware of every obscure detail of the scene. Dawn's face was framed by the black curly hair of her wig, which was now slightly unkempt and askew. Her neck hairs were darker and longer than usual, her fingernails chipped and unpainted because of her hospital stay and the lack of time and care that she usually had to put into her appearance. The two little empty communion cups were still sitting on her tray table beside some greeting cards that had come in the day's mail. The handmade paper sign on the wall behind her bed had her name written on it in blue magic marker: "Dawn Hastings." I was conscious of my unbroken eye contact and the degree of pressure with which I touched her hand and shoulder, and I realized in an instant that Dawn was watching me more closely than I had ever been watched by anyone before. I knew that she would sense immediately any shift in my demeanor: a wince, a blink, the faintest startled movement in my hands or body or facial expression; any quick eye movement away from her eyes and toward this intrusive, plastic, calibrated receptacle that now seemed ten times bigger than before.

Dawn looked at me and I looked at her with an unwavering gaze, wanting desperately to not give her any possible clue that I might find something unusual in this rich pastoral moment. This was a test. A test of acceptance, a test of friendship, a test of love, and I was determined to pass it. I continued to touch her and smile at her in the exact same way as I had done before the nurse came between us with "it." Who would speak first, now that I knew that she knew that I knew? In the course of my ministry over the previous several years I had stood up for Larry, marched in the Pride Parade, stuck my neck out with colleagues and church people and learned to be particularly sensitive to people's issues, but never did I feel a deeper act of compassion for someone's most private and personal secret than I did with Dawn in that split second. Somehow, I knew that the two of us were standing together on the bedrock of her struggle for personhood, and it could be very solid or very tenuous, uncertain ground for her, depending on my response. I was in a trusted place. I had just had communion with her.

"Dawn," I said, with no hint that what had just come between us in that physical space would come between us relationally, "I'm really glad we had this time together. Thanks for asking me to come. If there's anything else you need, just let me know. I'll be checking on you." I squeezed her hand and patted her face as I stood up straight beside her.

"Thanks a million, Renee," she said with a broadening smile. "You are really special. Thanks for being my pastor." Dawn's words were a reply to the visit, yes, but so much more than that. She was actually saying, "Thank you for standing with me in my circle of pain. Thank you for not being turned off by me. Thank you for letting me be who I am. Thank you for bringing me the love of God."

Dawn has never once, since that day in the hospital, mentioned the urinal incident, or the circumstances of it, nor has she ever made any reference to her sexual identity or her issues around it. She didn't need to. She didn't want to. She didn't have to. It wasn't important to her, so why should it be important for me to bring it up? And so I never have.

And the chaplain never did come by to bring her the eucharist.

\* \* \*

Christians must move beyond a limiting mind set that sees the world as either straight or gay; where straights are the ones blessed, welcomed, affirmed by God and the church; where gays are condemned. As long as we are stuck in that remote worldview, the real-life issues of millions of people who do not fit that mind set will be invisible to the church and its healing potential. It is not the fault of those in the sexual minority community. The blame falls squarely on the mainstream church. We must take responsibility for it and move toward the reconciliation of *all* orientations.

PART III

# Presenting
# the
# Challenge

# CHAPTER 9

# Openness to New Truths

*"The New Testament does not say,*
*'You shall know the rules, and by them you shall be bound,'*
*but 'You shall know the truth, and the truth shall set you free.'"*
—John Baillie

We have just heard and seen footage from the lives of real
people. If you have been able to hold your traditional judgments
at bay while allowing these personal experiences to touch your
awareness, you probably are full of all manner of feelings at this
moment. Perhaps there is some cognitive dissonance going on
between what you have been taught by the mainstream church
and how that translates, or fails to translate, into the real world
for many people. Your sense of truth has been challenged. Now
it comes into dialogue with others whose experience is very
different from your own.

How do you hold truth? Do you hold it with hands clenched
and close to your body, or do you hold it with hands open,
palms facing upward, away from your body? That first clench-
ing grip is the one we use when we are determined to hang on—
to hang on for dear life—because we are afraid that if we don't,
we will lose hold of our truth and be washed away into oblivion
and moral chaos. And so that we will not abandon all that we

have come to believe, we cling tenaciously and fiercely as others bring their truths to share.

The second way—to hold tenuously—is more like offering. I offer you my piece of truth so that you and others will share yours with all of us, and together we will arrive at a greater picture of the truth. My vision isn't the whole picture, nor is yours or anyone else's. It is only in the sharing that we come to see the value in others' truth, and even after we give and receive what we have to offer in this company, we will still not have a completed portrayal of what *really is*.

It is in the context of this sharing image that I bring my challenge to the church. So many congregants are certain of the completeness of their individual or corporate piece of truth that the very thought of having to receive others' offerings is terrifying. And so they hug their rightness all the more tightly. What I am asking of people of faith is that they loosen the emotional and spiritual vise that clamps their piece of truth to themselves. If they do so, then their hands will be open to receive that which comes from other sources.

The first step, obviously, is to recognize that other persons *have* other truths, based on their place in society. We have just seen this in the stories in Part II. Without respecting the realities that others who are different from us offer, we will not be able to reach higher levels of truth.

I heard a Native American saying that emphasizes this point for me: "The more different we are, the more special a gift we are to the community."

This is a profound teaching, and one that the church needs to take to heart, because we most often tighten our grip against beliefs that come from persons who are the most different from ourselves. Wouldn't it be worthy for the church to be identified as a place where every person is received as a unique and special gift to the community?

It is hard for us to hold our truth tenuously in order for there to be an openness to receiving the gift of someone else's experiential truth. Yet it is the Spirit of Truth that calls us to do this. We think if we are asked to re-examine our beliefs, to open up something we hold dear, we will have betrayed truth. Not so. It is a temporary posture in the search for the higher truth. It is a worthy goal. If we are having difficulty doing this, it is because we do not have enough faith in the God whose Spirit moves us beyond ourselves and our own horizons.

I dwell on the experiential aspect of reality because we have paid so little attention to it as a valid means of measuring truth in the tradition of the church. It is one of four specific tests that sincere churchgoers use to evaluate incoming data in order to discern truth. These tests are references to scripture, tradition, reason, and experience. In the mainline churches we want to begin and end every dialogue with a scripture reference. The result is that we are very good at quoting scripture. The problem with this proof is that scripture is misleading in the area of homosexuality and completely silent on other aspects of gender identity. There are so many disagreements as to what the truth of scripture is that we cannot use it conclusively to prove or disprove anything on this topic.

We are also very good at relying on the traditions and reason that seem to be based on scripture. But we have seen that none of these alone or combined is adequate to construct an approach or a moral code for sexual minorities. It is because of this that the church needs to be open to the critique that we are *not* very good at incorporating a wide spectrum of divergent or non-mainstream *experience* when it comes to forming our beliefs in certain areas. This is most apparent when looking at the issue of sexual variance.

The test of experience, as it comes from inborn sexual variance, has not been applied as valid alongside the other three proofs of scripture, tradition, and reason. Yet when we look at the life experience of our brothers and sisters with gay, lesbian, bisexual, and transgendered orientations, we find that there is a great and widening gap between what these first three tests are saying about "homosexuality" and what these persons are living every day in their individual maps of reality.

How do we solve this? Why is it even important to try? Because there are literally millions of people who are alienated from our communities of faith due to a knee-jerk condemnation based primarily on selective scripture, tradition, and reason. The pieces of truth held by those with inborn, minority orientations in the gender community are not being acknowledged or valued by the church, so why should they bother with the church? Yet, so many of them want and need the church.

Is this what the church—a movement begun by the great includer and lover of people, Jesus—was meant to be? A place that excludes and hates? If we were to search the scriptures to begin the test of truth for this reality of hate and exclusion, where would we go? How would we justify this? It is impossible. This should register an "Uh-oh" in our collective minds and send us to search the horizon for a way to reconcile this cognitive and spiritual dissonance, so that we can say at last, "Aha! I now see a larger picture of the truth." This is an ongoing process in the lives of faithful people.

I have shared the stories of twelve persons who are yearning for God and the church of Jesus Christ. They have all borne the brunt of scripture, tradition, and reason tests. It is time for us to lift our hands, release the fists of fear and hate, and hold our truth tenuously in a new posture of openness as we receive their experiential gift of truth.

It is this truth that will make us free—to love, to accept, to grow in the Spirit. But we have a choice as churchgoers. There are Christian people whose hatred, bigotry, and judgment will try to win us over—to tell us that Christian truth includes such things—to try to get us to behave in vindictive and exclusive ways in the name of religion. But the church is *not* a place for such things. This type of thinking and believing is wrong and life-destroying. It leads to the church being identified with office workers who jeer at gays in a parade, intolerant brownshirts, thugs who murder innocent people in the park, and parents who disown their children. Are these the consequences of a church teaching that we want represented or promoted in the greater society? I don't think so. The church is rooted in the sacrificial love of Christ, which could never be associated with a spirituality that would attack, hate, or abandon people in their pain.

We have a choice as Christians. The Jesus I follow shows me what choice I must make. I choose love, and that is the choice that will most cause me—no, *force* me—to grow in Spirit and in truth.

## CHAPTER 10

# The Pain the Church Doesn't See

*"It is so much easier to tell a person what to do
with his problem than to stand with him in his pain."*
—David Augsburger

## Pain in the Church

It's all around us. And most of the time, we do not, will not, or cannot see it. The pain of feeling excluded, unwelcome, condemned, is what keeps countless men and women—alone in their struggle, alone in their spiritual journey—from entering the doors of the church, when they need it more than anyone can imagine. What would make them want to come? What would make anyone want to come into a place where they would be spotlighted, singled out, and asked to deny or change who they are, or to be absolutely silent about all of it? And so, in order to find a welcoming, supportive community, some gay, lesbian, bisexual, and transgendered persons end up in a gay bar or bathhouse, or they may choose to escape the pain by turning to self-destructive behaviors. Alcoholism in the gender community is 300 times the national average; suicide is four times as frequent, according to PFLAG (Parents and Friends of Lesbians and Gays). The root cause of these evils is not homosexuality or other sexual orientation, but a church and society that force gay, lesbian, bisexual, and transgendered persons to want to escape hatred and judgment. Most of the time the church is totally unaware of the toll in human suffering and ecology.

I imagine that most pastors step in front of the congregation on Sunday morning, look across the variety of faces, and never think twice about sexual orientation. The reasons that orientation is not an issue for the pastor may be homophobia, fear, ignorance, or unresolved sexual-theological issues, which keep thoughts of homosexuality at a distance. Beyond this, clergy are most often totally unaware of those who are gay, lesbian, bisexual, or transgendered, because those people are silent. We can certainly understand the reason for the silence from the gay, lesbian, bisexual, or transgendered person's perspective. But this poses a problem, because the quiet, invisible one is utterly alone in his or her pain. The congregation is not in a posture of either receiving the special gift of truth and talent that this person brings or being able to share freely the struggles that are brought together during corporate worship. This unfortunate situation continues unchanged as long as the church is condemning of sexual minorities and as long as the pastor assumes that everyone seated in the pews is heterosexual.

What is the pastor not seeing in the faces of the worshipers? In that average congregation on a typical Sunday morning there may be persons who are having thoughts such as these:

"What if I am really gay? I'll kill myself so my parents won't have to do it."

"How can I possibly tell my church friends that my daughter just came out to me as a lesbian?"

"I wonder if anyone guesses that Jane and I are more than just roommates?"

There may be other persons sitting nearby who have no indication that such thoughts are going on. In fact, they are having other thoughts. In some congregations, for example, there may be some "little old lady saints" who, in their innocence, will whisper to one another about one of our gay couples. "Look at those two nice young men over there. So handsome. We need to find them two nice, pretty young women," they say as they begin the matchmaking process.

There may be conversations with someone, asking about his wife and family who are all at home with the flu, yet there is no question of concern toward the woman whose lesbian partner has just suffered a heart attack, because she can't talk about it in the same way. Here again we operate so much on assumptions that we are leaving our pew neighbors sitting in torment, without even realizing it. We assume that we know just by looking at someone what is going on with them sexually: in their thoughts, in their emotions and relational life, in their external genitalia, and in their behaviors. I have come to appreciate one huge new truth in the past few years: We cannot assume anything about anyone's sexuality. I will not ever be able to look at a man and a woman standing together in an affectionate way and assume that they are both heterosexual and attracted to one another. I will never again assume that the ordinary-looking woman in the back row is anatomically female. I cannot presume that, just because Jack is dating Cathy at the moment, they are both straight. There will be transgendered people and bi-sexuals who don't feel acceptable to anyone and who would be the last persons in the world to talk about any of their issues to the pastor or other church people.

All these examples and more are representative of what is actually present in our sanctuaries on Sunday morning and none of it is acknowledged or discussed in any way because most of us, beginning with the pastor, assume that everyone around us is heterosexual. However, in any given congregation, we must become aware that a certain percentage of people will have a non-heterosexual orientation. The current fuss and debate about whether or not "gays" should be welcomed into the church must seem perfectly absurd to those gay, bisexual, and transgendered people or their family members who are already in our pews and pulpits, paying the agonizing price of silence. This is the anonymous group in every congregation that is watching, waiting, yearning for some openness to be achieved in this area, hoping that someone in a leadership role will risk saying the word "gay" out loud during worship or printing it in the weekly bulletin in a positive way. The members of this group wonder how long it will be before there is even a glimmer of recognition of their presence.

At the same time there is a very intentional movement in some denominations and places of worship to seek out and change those "gays" who are there, to make them straight and acceptable or else to close the doors to them. The strategy is that, by taking such an approach, these homosexuals will leave their orientation behind and find true happiness by being straight (or, at the very least, celibate), and the church will help them to do it. This method has been used by leaders who then proclaim their success in terms of numbers of people "converted" or changed. I do not deny the transformed experience of many of these persons. That may be their lived truth. But it cannot or should not be everyone's truth among those who are non-heterosexual.

In most mainline churches, denial of the presence of gay, lesbian, bisexual, and transgendered persons is by far the predominant mind set. In fact, this is usually the case unless someone in the congregation has a reason to confide in the pastor, and that is more likely to be a confession that the parishioner's son or daughter is homosexual, and what should they do about it? The pastor who commonly assumes that everyone in her or his parish is straight and has straight family members is taken off guard, has few or no resources with which to help the troubled person, and may not know where to turn for information or advice. Seminaries, the very institutions that prepare ministers for pastoral care and counseling, are woefully lacking in current information and direction.

I will often get a call from a pastor in the region (sometimes from out of state) who knows me or has a friend who knows that I work in this area. Although I am pleased to be of help at these times, it is troubling to me when the pastor calling me has really never thought about this issue in a meaningful way until this particular incident surfaced and has no idea how to approach it, because the church has not offered much in the way of constructive help beyond judgments, prohibitions, and stereotypes—and now there is a real live person—a *known* person, who is unwittingly bringing the issue to the forefront. The tone of voice used by such pastors on these occasions is often subdued and anxious, and it changes to great relief when I can assure them that there is a lot of help in the community and that I can point them toward it.

No wonder I was not surprised when, standing before the very first meeting of GLAD to welcome about sixty gay, lesbian, bisexual, and transgendered persons, I was greeted with incredulous expressions. "A pastor? Welcoming us? Speaking to us with love and affirmation? How can it be? Here in a church? Impossible!" These comments are perfectly understandable in light of what most of these people have suffered in the name of religion. They have come to expect only exclusion, hate, and condemnation, based, of course, on their own past experience. What would make them think that anything has changed?

Over the course of the past few years I have had occasion to visit worship services that have been prepared primarily by and for non-heterosexual persons. Some of them gather on Sunday evenings to pray, sing, listen to the Word, and praise God together. The setting is especially nurturing because no one there has to be either invisible or silent. Everyone is able to come and participate freely without fear of being singled out, excluded, or asked to change. The entire agenda is worshiping God together, and it is always perfectly apparent to anyone in the room how much the people in attendance love the church and the God they serve. The liturgy they prepare is consistently beautiful and moving, with much lay participation in reading, praying, speaking, choirs, liturgical dance, and musical ensembles.

When I take part in events such as this I am at once struck by the marvelous devotion and care with which the participants handle the sacred symbols and ritual articles of their faith (perhaps even more so because of the underground nature of the setting). At the same time, I am filled with grief that everyone cannot find this same sense of peace, joy, and freedom in the mainstream congregation. Because of the attitudes in regular church settings, countless numbers of faithfully committed people are forced to find other places and other folks who will provide welcome and acceptance for them in their spiritual journey. It is a commonality of pain, which has driven them away and brought them together in this sacred place, under these circumstances. Why do excluded and condemned people even bother with the church? I'll never know for sure, but it must be that they, at a certain point experienced some spark of the light and spirit of

Christ that refuses to be put out. I often wonder if I would be so persistent and dedicated.

The alienation encountered in our churches has taken its toll on those who have already given up on the institution. This is always so blatantly clear when I go to groups to speak about this. I remember making a presentation to an organization of gay health-related professionals. These people were all doctors, nurses, technicians, EMS personnel, and other medical practitioners. Beyond references to their own personal experiences of the church from the past, their questions and opinions about the church were fairly well thought out and informed. My being there to speak was an excellent opportunity for many of them to vent their feelings about the church and what it had done or not done for them, and they were quick to challenge me about this and seek my views. Even there, the audience seemed surprised that there could be a pastor from a mainline church who could accept and celebrate all orientations.

Another memorable group was one from a university. A room full of students shared their hurt with me about how it felt for some of them, growing up in the church or synagogue and not having any support whatsoever from a teacher, pastor, youth worker, parent, or other adult in the congregation during an extremely formative and vulnerable time. There was virtually no one they could go to about their struggle in coming out, and they, as did the health professionals, expressed a lot of old anger and resentment at the community of faith that was simply not there for them. I looked around the room at these quizzical young adults, head-banded, book-bagged, and sandaled, faces broken out with acne, and I couldn't help but fault the church and its pastors for intending to give these young people a start in life and in the church, but doing virtually nothing to help them through the most difficult struggle of their lives. How they managed to survive that period of time through junior and senior high school to break free into the college support group that brought them to this moment was beyond me, and I was grateful for every one of them.

In every part of every city and small town in the country, and in the world, there is a young person who is living quietly and fearfully. This person had parents who wanted the very best for this child and introduced her or him to family life and to the community of faith. Over time, quite apart from the best intentions of parents, church, and family, this good, gentle person came to a frightening realization: "I am gay." "What caused this?" they may wonder. "Why me?" "Why can't I be open about who I am? Why can't I be happy about it?" But the questions have no answers, because there are no good answers, any more than we know for sure how heterosexuality is caused. "Why doesn't the church accept me?" someone from a sexual minority asks, and there is no good answer for that either. In fact, in the church—perhaps more so than in the greater American culture—it is dangerous to risk honesty about being gay, because the church teaches, and far too many of its pastors believe, that it's a sin. How in the world will we get people of all ages who struggle with their sexuality to come to the church for answers to critical questions and for support during times of emotional crises if we can't even get beyond square one, when we operate on assumptions and faith tests that don't begin to speak to the life experience that informs those who struggle?

It is there—the pain. It is all around us. We are wearing collective blinders, and it is time for Christians to positively address the unseen pain before we lose more of the patience and devotion of countless numbers of the silent, invisible, and oppressed who wait with open eyes and ears to see and hear one word—just one—of love and acceptance from the church.

## Pain in the Community

An important thing to note when talking about the gay, lesbian, bisexual, and transgendered community is that the "community" phenomenon is not well-defined or long-established, and the pain there is collective in nature. When one speaks of the Jews or the Blacks or other "communities" there is a history connected with each of them as a "people." This happens even if, in general, the history of these groups has not gained equal prominence to white, male, European history, for example. At least in the Jewish and black communities there have been families, traditions, stories, and cultural treasures of various kinds that have been passed down from one generation to the next to impart a sense of history, family, and pride. In each of these other types of communities there have been heroes, role models, villains, and events that have helped to shape the members and to bring the particular community together as a "people." For gay, lesbian, bisexual, and transgendered persons, however, this has been sadly lacking—or, if there, intentionally hidden and erased by the popular culture.

For non-heterosexuals, the level of oppression is still such that the freedom to have "community" is very limited except in the larger cities. By virtue of the fact that most gay, lesbian, bisexual, and transgendered persons do not couple for the purpose of reproduction and form families and extended families as other groups do, it is much more difficult to form a "people" history, with its associated places of origin, pride, and tradition that make it feel like a community. And so, for sexual minorities, the concept of community must be lived out and experienced in a different way. History and role models must be found in different places, and the church and society in general must somehow be readied for this to happen.

The need for community is one that is so basic and important to all persons that homosexuals, transgendered, and bisexual people have moved to meet their need for community by having their own restaurants, bars, clubs, bathhouses, activity centers, support groups, newspapers, publications, organizations, and even churches.

Religious institutions could be at the center of the "community" where all people would be free to live out our shared history together, if it were not for the traditions and teachings that hold us back. If we, as the mainstream church, could see this, we could begin to address the communal pain of our brothers and sisters as they seek healthy role models and safe places to gather together.

CHAPTER 11

# Why Can't We See the Pain?

*"Wherever you see persecution,*
*there is more than a probability*
*that the truth is on the persecuted side."*
*—Hugh Latimer*

We in the church have failed to see the pain, and in doing so have failed the ones who are caught in it. We have not been there for them in positive, affirming ways. We have not given them the support they need in their search for solace and help. We have not offered support when they struggle as young people with their sexual identity, nor in their older adult years to provide guidance and fellowship. We have created a sometimes cruelly silent, sometimes openly hostile climate where people are terrified to come out as homosexual, bisexual, or transgendered. We have not encouraged committed, lasting relationships and have failed to provide any alternatives that will help persons of gay, lesbian, bisexual, or transgendered orientations to avoid unhealthy lifestyles. We have discriminated against or overlooked whole categories of people, and we have, nonetheless, maintained our rigid truth in the midst of all the pain. What keeps us from responding to this human suffering?

## Stubbornness

A big reason is stubbornness. We are so absolutely certain that we already know the truth about "homosexuality" and God's will for non-heterosexuals that we don't even bother to examine whether we might be wrong about our accepted beliefs. We in the church are so distracted by studying, arguing, and being angry and polarized with each other about whether scripture marks homosexuality as a sin that we have totally missed the breadth and depth of the issues and pain that continue to increase while we are somewhere else, sounding very unconvincing to the persons about whom the arguments are addressed. The church is so stuck in its contest of who does or who does not have the real truth about homosexuality that many gay, lesbian, bisexual, and transgendered persons have written us off and gone off to find their own framework for spirituality and moral development—one that takes gender variance as a given, with its particular struggles and questions. The church hasn't looked closely enough to even see it. The people being excluded are not waiting for us to settle our fight. For most gay, lesbian, bisexual, and transgendered persons, the whole debate is no longer relevant. They are living every day in a reality that is untouched by the church, because the institution is oblivious to those living in it.

This is especially true when the church confines the focus of its discussion merely to homosexuality. But what about bisexual and transgendered people? The church hasn't looked closely enough to see that the very term "homosexual" cannot possibly encompass all the variations of persons who are feeling alienated and injured by this fray of controversy. We haven't even noticed. It must seem to many millions of gay, lesbian, bisexual, and transgendered persons that the church is at least one hundred years behind, based on this one observation alone.

Perhaps, in another several generations, the church will recognize that the term "homosexual" so barely scratches the surface that we will be forced to recognize the inadequacies of our teachings in this area of sexuality. By that time, non-heterosexuals will surely have gone on to more helpful forms of spirituality that are more loving and accepting than the church—the very institution that itself claims to promote love and acceptance. Possibly, the non-heterosexual community will also then have the necessary confidence to boldly demand the church's rationale for its using scriptures to promote hate, fear, and exclusion, rather than love.

## Dualism

Another reason the church is blind to the collective hurt of gay, lesbian, bisexual, and transgendered persons is our adherence to the concept of dualism. Dualism refers to the two natures, body and spirit, interpreted by some scholars and church officials down through the ages to mean that "spirit" was good and "body" was bad. Anything having to do with the body, especially sensory, sensual, or sexual pleasure, was taught by the church to be inherently evil. Whereas it was thought that by denying one's bodily concerns, one could rise to a higher level of being—namely, that of spirit.

If one looks at scripture in a cultural context, it becomes evident that Paul's writings were so influenced by Greek thought that we cannot dismiss that fact as incidental. Trying to separate body and spirit was as difficult 2,000 years ago as it is now. Yet that is what some early interpreters of Paul taught and subsequent church preachers and interpreters of scriptures believed. When teachers the caliber of Augustine (who was steeped in Platonism and Manicheism) wrote volumes of text that promoted dualism, it became foundational for the church (and civil law) for many hundreds of years to come. It is seen in the present day, even though the church has divided into countless denominations, each with slightly different interpretations of Paul.

Where does this leave us today? It leaves us all struggling to integrate our spirituality with our sexuality in a way that is life-giving to both dimensions. The way we are embodied dictates in the most basic of all ways how our spirit is experienced and how we grow spiritually. Try to imagine living in this world completely divorced from your body. How absurd. We are not bodies having a spiritual experience, we are spirits having a bodily experience, and how we are embodied is absolutely basic to who we are spiritually. By denying our bodies and our earthly connections, we are trivializing our own human condition.

Now, imagine a gay man, lesbian, bisexual, or transgendered person struggling within this dualistic model of church teaching. These people are in a position where, in grappling to integrate sexuality and spirituality (as anyone would in the process of spiritual journey), they must not only go through the ordeal of coming out to themselves and others, they must also then denigrate their sexuality—suppress it, ignore it, hide it, change it—in order to be acceptable and compatible with this dualistic Christian teaching that doesn't allow sexual expression outside of heterosexual marriage.

It's time to challenge the whole concept of dualism as it applies specifically to gay, lesbian, bisexual, and transgendered persons. Of course, in doing so we must replace it with something that is morally sound. This problem will be addressed further in the next chapter.

## Stereotypes

The use of stereotypes can also blind the church to the tremendous pain experienced by non-heterosexual persons. How many times have we heard the phrases "the gay lifestyle" or "the gay agenda?" The idea that all gays share a similar lifestyle is as ludicrous as the idea that there is such a thing as a heterosexual lifestyle, or a female lifestyle, or a particular racial lifestyle. Yet the use of the term "gay lifestyle" is a common way of referring to certain behaviors of gay men, without having to say "promiscuity." The reason this "lifestyle" terminology is so damaging is that the stereotype applies to only a small fragment of the non-heterosexual community. Yet promiscuity is the only "lifestyle" that some heterosexuals can imagine from a gay man (lesbians seem to enjoy a little more grace in this area). Many heterosexuals, operating on stereotypes and assumptions, believe that all gay men engage in promiscuity by virtue of the fact that they are gay. Admittedly, it is a challenge to look beyond such thoughts when seeing mattresses on the back porch of a gay bar; however, that cannot and should not be equated with all gay men's behavior. What we can logically condemn is promiscuity—not homosexuality. Somehow it is impossible for rigid church people to see that there might be anything like healthy, stable, long-term coupling among non-heterosexuals, and this deficiency makes it difficult for them to enter into a friendly, consciousness-raising conversation about it.

Sometimes the erroneous stereotype includes not only the idea of promiscuity, but also other ruinous myths such as the belief that homosexuals are child molesters, or that if we allow gays to be open about their sexuality, they will try to "come on" to us or try to convert us. Other facets of the stereotype involve mannerisms and dress; still others have to do with the gay person's upbringing and childhood environment.

Such stereotypes are harmful because it is no more possible to generalize about homosexual orientation than it is to do so about heterosexual orientation. Is there promiscuity in the non-heterosexual community? Of course there is, just as there is in the straight world, and it is wrong wherever it is found. Are there non-heterosexuals who like to be swishy or butch? Yes, but we certainly cannot generalize about that any more than we can say that all women like to cook or all men like sports.

It is too bad that the media tends to reinforce some of these stereotypes. For example, when the Pride Parade is reported on the local news, the cameras zoom in on the flamboyant dressers and the persons who most enjoy the shock value of certain gestures and behaviors. Because these images are the ones that get primary exposure to the general public, it is little wonder that the ordinary people in the parade who do not make statements by the way they dress, and who do not go out of their way to be malcontents, or who do not try to be intentionally offensive— are not the ones who make the evening news. They are too common and even boring to be newsworthy. They are too much like people of every other type. They remind us too much of ourselves.

This practice of stereotyping is one of the biggest stumbling blocks for the Christian community when it comes to understanding the pain among gay, lesbian, bisexual, and transgendered persons. Getting past this obstacle will take tremendous spiritual energy. We must intentionality let go of pictures we hang onto that make us think we already know the truth about these things. This will not be easy, but we must—we *must* do it, or we will never be able to touch people in their innermost places of need.

## Sexism

One of the most pervasive and destructive realities in American society for straights as well as non-straights is the fact that we live within male-centered, male-identified, patriarchal systems, including the institutional church. Within the constraints of sexist, gender-based power structures all men, women, and children suffer, whatever their sexual orientation. In a society where males are valued more than females, several things happen. First of all, people (especially males) may try to clarify the differences between maleness and femaleness as a way of maintaining the higher-status gender stereotypes. Anything that is perceived as less than male (or more like female) is devalued. This is unfortunate because both males and females are then denied the full spectrum of human experience and potential. Men who wish to be expressive, emotional, and nurturing are as much at odds with the old stereotype as are the women who are aggressive, competitive, and physically forceful. When such atypical behaviors are evident in a person, the resulting incongruity with the norm is often described as "queer," "butch," or some other derogatory word.

It is the basest form of sexism, which demeans homosexual, bisexual, or transgendered men because they would lower themselves to act like women. The underlying question is, "Who would *choose* to behave like a woman?" If we lived in a society where males and females had equal value to begin with, then there would be little chance that one gender would be condemned for showing behavioral traits of the opposite gender. There may even be little differentiation between the actual behavioral traits of men and women because persons would be free to express the whole gamut of what we now consider to be male traits and female traits. We would all be free to be who we truly are without the constraints of sexism that our culture puts on us and perpetuates.

Fears associated with this kind of sexism put challenging obstacles in the pathway of a gay, lesbian, bisexual, or transgendered person's journey toward wholeness. It is not easy to determine which fears around gender are the most basic: a non-heterosexual person's fear of being bad, sick, or different and the associated consequences; or those same fears *about* gay, lesbian, bisexual, or transgendered persons that are held by heterosexuals. Then there are fears that gay, lesbian, bisexual, or transgendered people will somehow try to change heterosexuals or molest their children, or shift the power base away from the straight white male one that we have now. Here again is a place where the church must re-examine its theological bases for either going along with such fear and oppression or for failing to do anything about it in an age where the voices of liberation are arising from every corner of the world around us.

Sexism and its associated fears and complications present deep questions to the church, questions that go far beyond the responsible use of scripture, tradition, and reason.

## Fear of Difference

Why are we so afraid of things that are "different"? There is a discomfort that goes along with being face to face with someone who does not share our own world view, physical appearance, or culture. There may be some curiosity about such difference between people, especially when we are on a vacation or trip. In fact, we may go to other countries and continents simply to see the exotic and the different. But when we encounter them in "our" space and invading "our" traditions and culture, we get frightened and nervous. Our neighborhoods, work places, churches, and homes become well-defended as we struggle with fears around diversity and difference, especially evident around gender variation. Sometimes our "idea" of what a gay man, lesbian, bisexual, or transgendered person is like frightens us more that the real encounter. We may not yet have a face to go with the label, and that is often a first hurdle to overcome when dealing with sexual variation. I think back on my first conscious meeting with a gay man—John. I am sure that much of my discomfort had to do with the fact that I had no point of reference as I integrated this kind of difference into my map of reality.

Knowing that we may be sitting next to a bisexual or lesbian in a church pew may be scary for any number of reasons, but we—as people of the God who created variety and diversity—must be ready to overcome our fear of difference in order to reach out to fellow human beings in love and affirmation. Fear of difference is one area where congregations must work at not allowing our fears to interfere with our Christian mandate to love one another.

## Jesus' Teachings

Perhaps the sorriest reason that the church has failed to embrace gay, lesbian, bisexual, or transgendered persons is really a summary of all the others: we have not truly followed the Jesus described in the gospels—the one who shows us how to be radically loving and inclusive. In the name of religion we have hated, pushed away, condemned, and excluded, instead of embracing, loving and including. Jesus would be deeply offended and ashamed that the church—the inheritors of Jesus' own ministry—would be so full of self-righteousness, hate, and judgment. He never meant it to be this way.

Jesus brought a different message to the world. The image that captures it best for me is the one of the Great Banquet (Luke 16: 14–24 and Matthew 21: 2–10). Here we see a master being disappointed in the esteemed guests who had turned down his banquet invitation with one excuse or another, and so he sends his servants out into the highways and byways, into the streets and behind the hedges to find anyone and everyone with whom to share this wonderful feast. Imagine the people they would find. In Jesus' day this was a radical concept, because of an obsession with politics of purity. Jews weren't supposed to sit down with just anyone, let alone eat with them. Yet this is what Jesus was saying.

The image of the Great Banquet is not so radical in our day in one sense, because we have no universal religious purity laws to uphold. I can go to the fast-food restaurant next to my church any time of the day and see there a variety of people: students, medical personnel, vagrants, businessmen and -women, homeless, professional types, etc. The metaphor breaks down at this point because the important dynamic of the *intimacy* of the Great Banquet—sitting down in fellowship and celebration of one another at one large table—is missing from our picture of the fast-food restaurant. However, Jesus was so intentional about this idea of inclusive love and compassion that he was always in trouble with the religious authorities over it, and yet he continued to push the issue.

This is the kind of Jesus I want to follow: the one who loved so completely and so courageously that he was willing to die for those whom he loved. Troublemakers such as Jesus didn't last long in a strict socio-politico-religious system such as existed in pre-church Palestine.

Why can't the church follow Jesus courageously today? Why are we not willing to love, to include, to embrace and have compassion for those who yearn to feast with us? To be willing to die for those on the fringes of life? To share in the brokenness of Christ when we are persecuted for being like Jesus? To me, these are questions that should never exist—they should never need to be asked. The fact that I pose them now means that the church has failed to follow Jesus faithfully because we have let attitudes and doctrines blind us to the real issues lived every day in the world of gender-varied experience.

In spite of difference we can achieve intimacy and communion. But something must change, and it must be the institution church, not oppressed gay, lesbian, bisexual, and transgendered persons. This is what Jesus intended. This is what Jesus taught. How can we, therefore, justify excluding *anyone* based on inborn traits and orientation?

We can continue to spend our time debating about sin and Christian teaching and scriptural proofs for this and that, but meanwhile we are missing the chance of a lifetime to move beyond all that and engage hurting persons in truly meaningful ministry. Because we are not able to see the pain, many gay , lesbian, bisexual, and transgendered people have already written off the church, and they alone know how that feels. But there are many others who are waiting patiently for the church to move beyond stubbornness and dualism—to put aside sexism, fear of difference, and unfortunate and inaccurate stereotypes—and to take some bold, new, loving, Christlike leadership in this arena. But the church must do it now.

CHAPTER 12

# The Church Must Lead the Way

*"It's not how much you know;*
*it's what you do with what you know."*
—John Hunter

## The Church's Causative Responsibility

We live in a time when society in general is hateful and oppressive toward non-heterosexual persons. How did it get that way? Where did this attitude come from? It was fostered by the church itself, as it has debated about homosexuality over the centuries. For this discussion, we must bracket out all behaviors except that of homosexuals, since the church has recognized primarily this one non-heterosexual group so far.

### The Sin Model

Much of our present negative stance toward homosexual behavior comes from Judeo-Christian teaching, which came to this country with European colonists and pioneers as they settled across the land. As far back as the Middle Ages, early scriptural translations and interpretations caused certain cultural dispositions and mandates to come into being. For example, "sodomy" is a term derived from some interpretations of Genesis to refer to same-sex intercourse that still appears in civil law. Even persons not in the church will use the scriptural reference argument when defending a position of disapproval. It is fascinating to me that when I ask someone who has no connection with a church or community of faith why that person feels homosexuality is wrong, I am usually reminded that it is a sin according to the Bible. I don't think we realize how thoroughly the sin model coming from the Judeo-Christian ethic developed around homosexuality has permeated the whole of Western society.

The sin model cannot exclusively or adequately describe homosexuality. It is important to remember that that *all* persons—no matter what our sexual orientation—must be aware of our own sinfulness. God created human beings with the freedom to make choices—for good or evil. We make such choices about innumerable things every day, only a few of which involve our sexuality. Those who adhere to the sin model of homosexuality would claim that being a sexual minority in itself is a choice, and that it is an evil choice. The "good" person *chooses* to be heterosexual. Since, however, inborn homosexuality, bisexuality, and transgendered sexualities are not choices at all but orientations, the only moral choice is how to *use* sexuality, no matter what the inborn orientation might be. There are good, life-giving choices and evil, life-destroying choices open to all inborn sexual orientations. A person's orientation, in itself, is not life-destroying; it is not a sin. Sinfulness enters at the point when we make life-destroying choices about orientation. This is another reason why it is important to abandon the sin model as church teaching. The role of the church is not to condemn inborn gay, lesbian, bisexual, and transgendered persons as sinners, but to help them form the basis for good moral choices based on one's orientation—sexual givens that have nothing to do with choice.

### The Illness Model

At the turn of the century, when Darwin was doing his work from a genealogical perspective—proposing his survival of the fittest theory—some people working in the human sciences, who were influenced by his studies, concluded that homosexuality must be caused by a defective gene. The mind-set of the time was, then, to identify the homosexual as one whose constitution needed to be fixed, or cured. So doctors, psychiatrists, psychotherapists, and other's were likely to try to change the sexual invert to correct or heal the defective condition, through psychotherapy or medication, or by identifying some cause.

In the seventies both the American Medical Association and the American Psychological Association removed homosexuality from their lists of disorders. In doing so, the public medical community moved away from the illness model to the variance model, wherein homosexual persons are seen not as patients in need of healing solely by virtue of their sexual identity, but as variations within the natural order, with distinct features and potentialities. Meanwhile, the church, still adhering to the sin model, was left far behind the conclusions already reached by the human sciences.

While many church people continue to believe unwaveringly that homosexual behavior is a sin, some have moved from the sin model to the illness model. This is the basis for what is called the Exodus Movement, which calls for homosexuals to be changed, transformed, and healed, in other words—helped, forced, or coerced, to adopt heterosexual behavior. The unfortunate assumption of such movements is that *all* homosexual persons are able to change, given the proper approach. Some persons have changed their behavior (which is not convincing proof that the orientation has been altered.) But this change could indicate movement toward a true heterosexual orientation, and so it is impossible to generalize such experience to make it everyone's truth and to expect that this is a desired option for an inborn homosexual with a different truth.

I have met many persons who were casualties of such an approach because they were *born* a certain way and could not change. The person, unable to truly change, ends up feeling even more guilty and condemned. People who are gay can act straight, but that doesn't change anything about their underlying orientation. Furthermore, bisexuals who participate in this sort of process may be more able to conceal their true orientation because, on the surface, they couple as heterosexuals—which somehow "proves" that they have been transformed. So many people have told me about the anguish and duplicity this method creates that it is in many ways even more cruel than denouncing the homosexual person to begin with. Besides, in spite of statistics that are used to try to persuade us of the success of these procedures, there seem to be many more ex-straights than there are ex-gays!

If the secondary goal for Exodus-type movements is celibacy, then the rationale for such an expectation is elusive. If one is truly and irreversibly homosexual, bisexual, or transgendered, then why must we require celibacy? Is their sexuality not a good gift from God, just as anyone else's is? For many, the operative rationale is that a male and female coming together for procreative purposes is God's ideal plan for humankind. If this is true, then what about love—the unitive purpose in coupling? If love renders the unitive purpose as valid as the procreative, then why must we limit coupling to male-female partners? Further, where any person (heterosexual or otherwise) may choose celibacy for moral reasons, an equally valid moral choice for anyone—regardless of orientation—is coupled relationship.

As long as the church only recognizes heterosexual coupling as natural and good, we can continue to defend a moral code for heterosexuals and married couples, but we will be excluding an enormous population whose created sexual identity is neither sinful nor sick. We must see that there is yet another model, which will provide a better framework for understanding all types of sexuality.

### The Variance Model

The largest group within mainline American churches still adheres to the sin model. A smaller group is now dedicated to the illness model, which the medical community itself has moved beyond. The smallest group in the church today is where the medical sciences are—namely, that homosexuality and all other non-heterosexual orientations are simply a variation of God's natural created order. Supporting the variance model is a stretch for many churchgoers, but we must be there if we are to begin to address the pastoral issues that have existed in the gay, lesbian, bisexual, and transgendered community throughout all the time it has taken for us to move from one model to another. Variety is *God's* gift to us. But we haven't accepted it yet. These mind-sets or models represent points along a continuum, no one model being complete in itself. When insights occur, they provide us with movement along the continuum, allowing us to reincorporate and reconfigure our map of reality. The variance model is the point of celebration of difference.

Recognizing differences, moving to tolerance, arriving at acceptance, and finally celebrating diversity is, for some reason, as difficult as it is frightening. Yet this is what the church *must* be about, as we consider our relationships with people of varying sexual identities. We have had to learn to appreciate diversity in the areas of racial, ethnic, and gender inclusiveness. The church must push beyond the sin model regarding homosexuality because it is not accurate or adequate. We must, likewise, get past the illness model for the same reasons. True affirmation and celebration can only come when we allow ourselves to understand and accept the variance model and see that each person—regardless of how they are embodied—is a beautiful and unique gift from God exactly as she or he is created.

### *Transitional Attitudes*

As the church struggles to embrace a more inclusive and loving model, the transition from old attitudes to new ones is also reflected in the secular non-heterosexual community. Everyone who is gay, bisexual, or transgendered does not agree on how to approach the vast diversity among themselves. In some communities, for example, lesbians are less valued than gay men, bisexuals less still, and transgendered persons the least valued and accepted by the other groups.

Some non-heterosexual persons want to take a separatist stance, where they and they alone empower themselves. As malcontents, advocates, and role models, they push against the heterosexual world to find their own strength and direction. Others work hard at reconciling the differing groups, providing education, social opportunities and networking. In previous years this networking aspect was "headquartered" in the gay bars—a safe place for "community" where all social action, fund-raising, and organizational constituencies were located.

At present, much loyalty to the gay bars and businesses still exists, but there are many more choices opening up. In a gay newspaper, for example, one can find wonderful articles about the many positive things happening in the subculture, about celebrities and causes, and new groups one can join, about personal relationships, AIDS, legislative matters, and the need to be accepting of diversity even among non-heterosexuals and races. At the same time, however, one can often find a whole section of the paper that borders on pornographic material. In this transition time within this subculture, the same vehicles that are used to do very wholesome and uplifting things for people in various stages of coming out are also the ones where the worst possible face of sexual behavior is promoted and reinforced because of the substantial profits that are involved in this type of material. (Even our widely read city newspapers are not immune to this. Note some of the semi-pornographic material found in the sports and personals sections of our major city newspapers.)

Unfortunately, the bad comes with the good. When our ecumenical group GLAD has an activity that needs widespread publicity and support from the gay community, we must use gay newspapers that include all of that. One time, after an outside group had used our church, one of these newspapers was inadvertently left behind and found by one of my church members, who was shocked and outraged by what she saw on some of those pages. She brought this matter to the attention of some of the church leaders and I was asked to explain, defend, and interpret what this was all about. It is very difficult to convey to church people what is going on in the gay, lesbian, bisexual, and transgendered community regarding sexual lifestyles. It is not easy for them to understand that there are a variety of attitudes and approaches coming from the subculture that not all gay, lesbian, bisexual, and transgendered persons will necessarily feel the same way about what is available to them from their own peers. Churchgoers find it difficult to understand this phenomenon because the church itself is so divided on these issues. Of course, there will be a shadow side in every culture, but if there are only one or two gay newspapers in the city, and they print whatever is asked of them simply because it is profitable to do so, then those newspapers will contain uncensored and undesirable material along with everything else. This is yet another place where reinforcing stereotypes and generalizations (about promiscuity and other issues) only serve to get us further away from seeing where the real needs are. If we could realize that in many places, the non-heterosexual community has precious few resources for reaching people and promoting healthy choices and networking, we could be there, as people of faith, to help develop positive, value-centered materials that would have a powerfully beneficial effect on the entire community.

One way GLAD has helped to do this is by coordinating an annual activity called Info-Fest, where about seventy gay-friendly organizations, agencies, religious groups, and businesses come to the church and set up a display with literature and contact people who can talk about and promote the group. Persons from all over the Pennsylvania-Ohio-West Virginia area come to find information and networking that they can't find anywhere else in one place. And it is located—of all places—in a church; a church that cares about people and about how they find their way in a confusing world that sometimes has conflicting signals and values. But the need for such information and affirmation is obvious. How many other regular church activities draw 400 people with such enthusiasm and gratitude?

## The Church's Corrective Responsibility

### *Reexamining Our Moral Code*

Before the church can make a real difference in embracing all sexual orientations, we must reexamine our moral code and realize how woefully lacking it is as we address the needs of our gay, bisexual, and transgendered sisters and brothers. If we look closely at the Bible, we will see that we really do not have a clear sexual ethic. In certain scriptures, we find men of God who have many wives, slaves, and mistresses with whom they are allowed to have sexual relations in order to promulgate the chosen race.

There are women of God who solve the problem of barrenness by lying with in-laws, out-laws, or incestuous partners. Serial monogamy appears as a model in some settings, as well as a mandate not to marry at all, unless the urgency of lust proves too much to bear. Adultery occurs in high and low places, and divorce seems to be an option for a variety of reasons. Sperm is never, never to be wasted because it is needed to increase the people of Israel, and so laws against masturbation and non-procreative intercourse were put forth for males. (It seems that females are more exempt from these last prohibitions.)

If we try to extrapolate from the entirety of scripture a single, clearly defined sexual ethic, we find that it is virtually impossible. Yet that is what we want to claim that we, as people of Judeo-Christian heritage, have managed to do. What we seem to have is a conglomeration of dualistic injunctions that aim to keep our bodies "pure" by strictly controlling our sexual activity within the confines of heterosexuality—marriage is the only place where sexual relations are allowed; singleness assumes a heterosexual orientation; coupling is always assumed to be heterosexual in nature. All other expressions of sexuality are defined as sinful, sick, and even abominable, yet there is still confusion around the Christian purpose of marriage and sexuality in general: what is natural; what are procreative versus unitive purposes; how do these issues play out when making decisions whether or not to use birth control, etc. But the church has grown to accept and promote new teachings denouncing incest, polygamy, and slavery as sinful, in spite of scriptural arguments that prove these same things acceptable—even virtuous. This means that the Holy Spirit continues to move through our present truth as we grow toward greater truths. It is time that we opened ourselves to the movement of the spirit to develop new traditions and moral codes for non-heterosexual persons.

How do our gay, lesbian, bisexual, and transgendered brothers and sisters fit the profile of persons who can relate to our present moral code? They don't. They can't. Some will disregard the entire set of mandates because they simply do not apply. (Perhaps these are the desperate persons who seek out anonymous sexual encounters on the back porch of that downtown bar and countless other places.) Others will try to live by the sacred laws and deny who they are created to be (in which case the greater moral question is whether or not pretense is a worthy state of being). Still others will try to invent their own moral code when situations arise, because there is nothing to give them guidance. In this case, what is invented may come from popular myths, scraps of memories from old Sunday School teachings and sermons, values learned from family or friends, or bits and pieces of folk wisdom and leftover moralisms from the popular culture. People of ordinary ability are asked to accomplish the extraordinary feat of putting together a set of moral guidelines that honors the God who created us and the persons with whom we share our lives—all without theological training. Who will be their teachers? Will the hundreds of thousands of gay, lesbian, bisexual, and transgendered persons who go to their computers in the privacy of their bedrooms every night invent this moral code in chat groups across the Internet? Why are we not there to help?

It is critical that we in the church realize that millions of genuinely good persons are struggling to live moral lives, without positive cooperation and assistance from the religious community in this task. If we accuse them of taking a "Cafeteria Christian" approach to the teachings of the church, we must realize that we have not really given them alternatives that are relevant to their inborn experience. We must also realize that some of the choices in their lives right now have nothing to do with the church. To criticize them for this without offering moral guidance consistent with how they are embodied is unconscionable.

Without the church taking an active role in formulating new moral imperatives based on the realities of inborn experience, the gay, lesbian, bisexual, and transgendered persons are on their own. One of the greatest goods that can come from the church working with non-heterosexual persons is that, in the absence of a biblical sex ethic, we can use scripture to help all of us identify a love ethic.

It seems more and more that specific rights and wrongs around sexuality are impossible. Every act happens within a situation and context that must be taken into consideration. So to prescribe, prohibit, or promote any particular behavior is not a worthy goal when considering the development of a moral code.

A better approach is to use very simple guidelines. Is this act now (or potentially) life-giving for me and the other person(s)?

Is this act now (or potentially) life-destroying for me or the other person(s)? The simplicity of such a code requires us to weigh each act and struggle with what it means to be life-giving or life-destroying, in the context of a specific time, place, and company.

For Christians, all laws are reduced to an underlying mandate of love: love for God, and love for neighbor as self. It is clear that the over-arching framework of the scriptural message is that of love. God is love; God loves the world; Jesus came to manifest that love to humankind; we, who follow Jesus and seek God's will, love the Divine and our human neighbors as ourselves. Love is the first and second great commandment. The church must really believe that and teach that. It is this love that helps us to decide what is finally life-giving and life-destroying. (See the Appendix for authors whose work addresses the need and the framework for a new moral code.)

But we must first work from within the variance model of acceptance in order to put aside our misguided model based on the so-called "sin" of inborn homosexuality, in order to get on with really being the church in a pastoral, ethical, loving way.

How can we help people such as Lisa and Charlene—victims of a culture that expects them to marry and have children? Is it not a greater moral travesty to pressure inborn homosexuals into marriage and children, when the dishonesty, duplicity, and pain eventually affect all persons involved: wife, husband, children, in-laws, and friends? Would it not be infinitely more "moral" to affirm diversity of sexual orientation that assumes nothing regarding coupling or procreation? Why must we cause basically moral people to live a lie, only to accuse them of being grossly immoral when they then become honest and try to find ways to live out their orientation?

Couples such as Kathy and Claire and Stewart and Tim could turn to the church for guidance and support in their search for a moral code that affirms them, and they could be united as couples with the blessing of the church. Obviously, the church must first be in a corrective stance regarding the harmful traditions we have taught for so long before we can advocate for the acceptance of sexual variance within church and society.

### *Owning Responsibility*

The Judeo-Christian ethic has had a substantial causative responsibility for the way that homosexuals and other non-heterosexual persons are oppressed and treated in our society. Since inaccurate and misconstrued church teachings and traditions are the point of reference even for the unchurched members of society on this issue, then it is the church (enlightened pastors, teachers, theologians, bishops, and laity) that must assume corrective responsibility for the healing of the oppression and mistreatment of gay men, lesbians, bisexuals, and transgendered people.

The church must say to society, "We were wrong. We have looked again at our position and have found it to be inconsistent with the loving mandates of scripture, which are more central to the Christian message than anything that can be used to oppress, hate, and exclude. We apologize for all the hurt, injustice, and suffering that has occurred in the name of religion, and we will take the lead in modeling Christ's love and compassion to correct what we have allowed to happen in church and society."

If the church doesn't say this on its own behalf, who will? Who has the ecclesial power to remove the socio-religious bias against homosexual persons, which has existed for several hundred years, except the church? (Even better: the church in collaboration with other religious traditions such as Reform Judaism, Unitarian Universalism, and other religious groups.) Who else can adequately undo the scriptural interpretations on this subject if it isn't the church itself? No one has the same authority to do that. The church must do it. The church must see this. We must develop new study tools to transform our stance and thus transform society's stance as well. The only way society can be truly free of the old judgments based on scripture, tradition, and reason is for the church to step forward and forge a new way. It is the only foundational institution that can absolve the guilt that will arise when people begin to depart from teachings that have been used to condemn and oppress homosexuals and other non-heterosexual orientations. Only if the church takes responsibility for causing this problem in the first place can we create an environment wherein correction can begin.

### *A Starting Point*

What is the theological starting point for the needed correction? Where do we find a basis for beginning this process? Some people would look to the Creation stories in Genesis (ironically the same place I went in my seminary days to "prove" that homosexuality was a sin). There they would find that God created the world and everything in it, and that God pronounced it all "good." God created each of us the way we are, and the natural goodness of the created order allows us to know that God is a continual part of the process.

Another rhetorical strategy is to refute the condemning scriptural passages by presenting new interpretations: those from a gay liberationist perspective that show how to use scripture to free gay, lesbian, bisexual, and transgendered persons from oppression and condemnation. Still another approach that begins in scripture is to open up the whole question of the authority of the biblical witness and wording.

The healthy questioning and struggling with all that is handed down to us—whether it be scripture, tradition, or reason—is necessary to the strengthening of our faith as we integrate it into our experience. This is what the stuff of life is all about. If our faith is strong enough, it should not have to depend on  passed-down "certainties" that, on closer examination, are really not so certain after all. It is better that it be dependent on the Holy Spirit moving in and through all of what is available to us, not just particularities that, in the end, are the very things that prevent us from greater truth and understanding.

Scriptural strategies are important for the opening up of the church to its corrective responsibility. Certainly, for many people, if the scriptural arguments are not addressed, they will not take part in any discussion of the issue. But new insights and enlightenment will not come solely or primarily through scriptural debates. That is precisely where the church has lost immense amounts of time—locking horns over the Bible. We will never make progress if we confine ourselves to this approach.

Another strategy looks to the moment of baptism in the life of every Christian. If we take our theology of baptism seriously, we are saying, with every infant, child, and adult, of whatever sexual orientation who pass through the waters, that this person is claimed by God as a unique and beautiful child, with gifts, graces, and for ministry as part of the community of faith. As this person grows in faith, she or he grows in faithfulness to God's call and is destined to serve God in great and small ways through the life of the church. How can we tell them that they are not allowed to participate fully in any part of the life of the church, including leadership positions for laity or clergy? This was the predicament that John, Doug, Rich, and Nicholas found themselves struggling with as baptized Christians called to ministry.

The church is in a time of enormous tension between tradition and the changing culture. For some, challenging the sacred traditions means we are headed for chaos, wherein there will be no moral code, no touchstone of common Christian belief to pass down to future generations. But for others caught in the shadow side of tradition, there is an entrapment, a confining of the Holy Spirit, an irrelevance to life and everyday experience. This is where our gay, lesbian, bisexual, and transgendered sisters and brothers find themselves, and they cannot, they may not undo this on their own.

In order for the church to move to corrective action and direction, the loving, moveable middle must be persuaded that we are now so far off track that it will take a monumental effort to reclaim our credibility with those who have been excluded from the community of faith. Heterosexuals in the church must be educated and brought to a place of advocacy for non-heterosexuals. Gay men, lesbians, bisexuals, and transgendered people cannot accomplish this without heterosexual allies, and as long as we are silent, horrible human casualties will continue to be recorded in the form of suicide, hate crimes, life-destroying situations, and injustices. Liberation of an oppressed group hardly ever happens from the bottom up, unless it involves some kind of revolution, and I don't see a gay revolution happening in the church any time soon. It is too dangerous. Besides, what would be the point in setting themselves up for that kind of turmoil on top of everything else? Liberation will happen only when those who have the power to oppress come to realize the injustice of their ways and take corrective action.

It is time to point the finger of responsibility where it belongs—toward persons in the religious community (especially bishops, pastors, and theologians) who judge, condemn, exclude, hate, and oppress those with non-heterosexual orientations in and around our congregations. It is time to name our own sin of heterosexism and come to the place of repentance so that we can move forward into redeeming and corrective action. We have been locked into seeing the issue of "homosexuality" within the sin model, and we have been blind to the fact that we ourselves are the ones who live within the sin model. Heterosexism is *our* sin.

### A Worthy Vision for the Church

If only this could happen one day: If only the church could make the drastic changes within itself and then within our culture that are necessary for the celebrating of gender differences. Then the average pastor could step in front of the congregation on Sunday morning, look across the variety of faces, and never think twice about sexual orientation. Why? Not because the pastor is totally unaware of those in the room who are in a silent sexual minority. No. It would be because differences are more than recognized or feared or resented or tolerated or even accepted. It would be because the rich variety of sexual lifestyles is assumed.

In fact, my vision for the church is that we will arrive at a point some day where gender differences are genuinely celebrated and *embraced.* Church folk will ask people such as Stewart, Lisa, and Russell about their partners and warmly greet them when they arrive together in worship. José, Betty, and Dawn will feel valued and loved as they participate in the life of the parish. The words "gay" or "lesbian" or "bisexual" or "transgendered" will be mentioned positively in sermons and bulletins and brochures. Rainbows will appear on banners and clergy vestments.

Activities and support groups for all persons, regardless of sexual orientation, will be an integral part of the ministry of the church. Parents, friends, and other loved ones will be free to talk with pride about the special gay, lesbian, bisexual, and transgendered people in their lives. No one will fear coming out to the pastor or anyone else in the congregation because the church is inclusive and celebrative of all persons. Positions of leadership will be held by persons of every gender orientation. No job will be off limits for anyone because of sexual variance. Even the youth group will incorporate this affirming attitude and approach.

Is this too much to ask of the church of Jesus Christ? Is this not a worthy vision that we can capture and live out? Is this not the Great Banquet that Jesus told us about? Is this not an opportunity of cosmic proportions? Yes! Let's hope it is not too late. Our culture is already moving in a liberationist direction along the continuum—from the sin model to the illness model and then to the variance model. It is only a matter of time—perhaps a very long time, before there is true freedom from hate and oppression for gay, lesbian, bisexual, and transgendered persons. But think how much faster the movement could be if the church were to take responsibility for the leadership of this endeavor. The culture may accomplish social and political liberation, but only the church can pronounce freedom from *religious* oppression. Such freedom would then lead to spiritual liberation for *all*. Wherever there is any kind of exclusion, hate, tyranny, and brokenness, that is precisely where the church should be leading the way, not following behind.

Let us move boldly forward as the church of Jesus, the lover of all, to claim our responsibility for causing institutional pain within church and society for millions of gay, lesbian, bisexual, and transgendered people, and then find ways to correct the situation by accepting the variance model of sexuality, revising our moral code and including all sexual orientations at the Banquet of Life. God has already given them a seat at the feast. It is time for the church to do so as well.

CHAPTER 13

# A Word about Trust

*"Where the spirit of the Lord is, there is liberty."*
*—2 Corinthians 3:17*

Trust is a hard thing to come by in the gay, lesbian, bisexual, and transgendered community. It is a very precious gift that is only given when the recipient seems able to handle that trust with utmost care. It is a tremendous responsibility. It is not to be taken lightly.

When lesbian, gay, transgendered, and bisexual persons come openly to the church, it will be only when they sense that we really have repented of our heterosexism and have come to a place where we are making the world and the church radically different than ever before.

It will not come quickly. It will not come easily. This trust will have to be earned and built and negotiated over time. We in the church do not deserve to be trusted until we can prove that we really are as loving as we say we are; as accepting as we claim to be; as inclusive as we picture the Great Banquet to be. So far, we have not been faithful to any of these as applied to non-heterosexuals, and it will take persistent patience, care, and pastoral energy to undo all the pain and oppression that we have caused throughout time. All the while we will be carefully watched by gay, lesbian, bisexual, and transgendered persons to see if there is the slightest chance that we will fall back into our old ways, betraying our trust and proving that we could not pass the test after all. The church has come to symbolize such negativity and hate, legalism and self-righteousness, that to overcome these we will have to over-correct at first. This means we will have to be intentional as we start out, going the extra mile to use energy in our congregations and in our communities, families and work places to make the world safe and loving for those whom we have pushed away and silenced for so long.

Trust is a very big gift, one that we hope to earn by being the Christ in the world. There is a cost for this. Christ paid the ultimate price. We, as his followers, can do no less. We may have to suffer the discomfort of tension, confrontation, and loss of members and financial support in order to be the church that earns this trust. But we must not allow our fears of these eventualities hold us hostage to our sin of heterosexism. If faced with a choice between following Jesus and following the church, we must follow Jesus.

Only by loving in a sacrificial way will we have earned the right to be trusted by those who stand to be liberated by our actions.

CHAPTER 14

# A Word About Heresy

*"There is no disagreement greater than one
which proceeds from religion."* —*Montanus*

Because I have articulated my position regarding gay, lesbian, bisexual, and transgendered persons in various settings, I have been given a variety of names, all intended to discredit me and discount my views. These names include Gnostic, Liberal, Radical, Activist, and Malcontent Feminist. I suppose I knew this would happen as soon as I began to identify with this issue. From time to time I shake my fist at God and demand to know why I have been called to do this. I would never voluntarily choose to alienate peers, colleagues, and superiors .

Why would I do that? Why would I get up in the morning and say to myself and the world, "Today I will go against Christian teaching. I will defend a point of view that is colossally unpopular. It will be dangerous sometimes when I am threatened. I will probably receive hate mail, and it will likely have a detrimental impact on my career as a Christian minister. Church people will confront me and scrutinize my time and demand to know why I think I should be doing this."

Yet this is the irony. I have been questioned about whether I spend too much time working with people who have no central place in the life of the church. Even though some persons are involved in our congregation *because* we have ministries to and with all sexual orientations, others feel these ministries violate church policy and wish we would end all gay-related events. A line has sometimes been drawn between two points of view: one that welcomes homosexuals and one that welcomes *and* affirms the practice of homosexuality. The key word is *practice.* The tension along this line has surfaced on occasion, and has yet to be addressed in depth. I have unwittingly become a lightening rod person for this issue and it sometimes causes great stress, in spite of the goodwill and support of many parishioners.

The approval I have gained from my congregation to do this work has been, for the most part, unspoken and conditional. My involvement is not often questioned, but when the subject comes up it is usually couched in a discussion about how I use my time, or how certain parishioners might feel about specific things, or what I do at the expense of the "mainstream" congregation. Some parishioners are supportive as long as this doesn't cause a big controversy in the church; as long as no one gets disturbed and leaves the church; as long as our church does not become widely known as the "gay" church; as long as the timing of an event doesn't raise eyebrows from the leadership of the church; as long as I don't embarrass anyone.

Why would I set myself up for this kind of agony? At times, I think I can begin to know what it must be like to live a schizophrenic life—balancing between what I need to do to keep from having ecclesial charges brought against me for my beliefs and teachings, and the truth that I have come to know by relating to and serving persons of all sexual orientations.

The upshot of all this is that the most onerous name I have been called by some of my colleagues in ministry is "heretic." I must admit that hearing this word used against me has caused me terrible pain and alienation. Once, in preparation for a regional denominational meeting, I thought it might be good to look up the word "heresy," so that I could prove I was *not* a heretic. To my surprise, Webster's definition, in essence, was this: "An opinion…"—notice the word *opinion*—"which differs from traditional church teaching." I read it again. And again. "An opinion—" well, it definitely is an opinion—of mine and many others—"which differs from church dogma—" it certainly does differ in major ways.

I could only conclude from reading this that I can, in fact, be branded a heretic. However, at the same moment I was wonderfully empowered by the thought that being labeled a heretic put me in good company: using this same definition, Jesus could also be branded a heretic, and Martin Luther and John Calvin and John Wesley and lots of other religious reformers and theologians throughout history. Having had this revelation, I could then go to the meeting prepared to be called a heretic, but also prepared to defend my stand as a devout follower of Jesus who has called me to be part of the loyal opposition.

It occurs to me that it is not the use of the word "heresy" that is offensive to me. The content of the word can be easily disarmed. What is truly offensive is the very fact that someone would use that word against me or anyone else in the ministry of the church. "Heresy" is the ultimate distancing word. It means that we can't have church together any more. It means that we are disconnected as members of the body of Christ, whom we both love and serve, albeit in different ways. It is hateful and sanctimonious and the mere use of this word divides us more than any other act.

Who would ever have thought I would find myself in a place like this? Me—the naive one from Romeo, Michigan—the one who knew nothing about this, the one who learned from being scared silly by immersion in the real world and moved to compassion and advocacy; the one who is now being branded a heretic and facing the consequences of being in the loyal opposition. Incredible.

Those in the church who move forward into the challenge of corrective responsibility must be prepared for confrontation, polarization, and alienation, all in the name of religion. Persons who are holding on tightly to their piece of the truth, terrified to open up and let the Holy Spirit move among us with the larger truth, will react in volatile, perhaps vindictive and immature ways and work as obstructionists to what we are trying to achieve. That is part of the process. It shouldn't have to be that way, but it is.

PART IV

# Finding
# the
# Hope

CHAPTER 15

# Some Light Appearing
# on the Horizon

There is hope. There are some enlightened pastors and lay persons who have moved into the variance model of understanding gender identity. They are the ones who are at work trying to shepherd the church into the place where the Great Banquet image is lived out every day. They are the ones who, as we engage in dialogue together, have a faith strong enough to allow for a God who can encompass all the diverse points of view on this topic of sexual orientations. They are the ones who will finally bring about transformation in church and society.

At present, every major denomination within mainstream America has a movement whose purpose is to open the doors of church buildings to all persons, regardless of sexual orientation. This is a ray of hope for the Christian community and the world, and the light is growing brighter as word of this movement spreads.

Religious movements such as these are networking, collaborating, and forming partnerships with secular education and advocacy groups such as PFLAG (Parents and Friends of Lesbians and Gays), leagues of gay and lesbian voters, teachers, librarians, musicians, professionals, service providers, medical personnel and more. Often these secular groups are wonderfully surprised when church people—clergy and laypersons—offer their help, support, and facilities.

It is when pastors and lay persons start taking a stand for inclusion and affirmation of gay, lesbian, bisexual, and transgendered persons that people begin to talk about their own orientation or that of a family member or friend. As pastors come forward out of their anonymity to speak with other pastors of their concerns for their non-heterosexual brothers and sisters, so also will lay persons within a congregation come forward to speak their concerns to the pastor and other lay people when the opportunity presents itself in the local church.

It is because of this light on the horizon that I find hope as a clergy person called to work openly with persons of all sexual orientations. Many times I have wondered if I should leave my denomination for one that is already welcoming and affirming of all persons, regardless of sexual orientation. Or perhaps I should leave the ordained ministry. Why should I continue to push against the limits of tradition and acceptability within the mainstream church? Why should I keep subjecting myself, my congregation, and my colleagues to quiet and not-so-quiet confrontation? The answer is really another set of questions: If people who share my experience and, thus, my frustration with the institutional church would put down the struggle and leave it all behind, who would be left in the church to bring change? Who would be the pioneers to open the church to the Spirit of Truth brought by persons who genuinely yearn for the community of faith? No one. The spirit of judgment, hate, and exclusion will have won, and that violates every sense of the gospel that I know. It is my church, after all. Why should I have to leave it?

I have to believe that the true, loving church of Christ is out there—quiet, waiting, hopeful—people whose voices have not yet dared to speak, but who will break their silence to come forward if hospitality and affirmation are offered to persons of all sexual orientations. We need to be aware of this and to keep that ray of hope alive. We can and must continue the work that has begun. We can be the pioneers—the ones who lift up the light. And as we do, the world will be able to see it, and the light will, through persistence and compassion, become brighter and brighter as more and more people are touched by the love, compassion, and justice of Christ. He is the one who brought the light to the world. We are the ones who must never let it die.

Where is a church that is both welcoming and embracing? It's right here—in you and in me. *We are that church!*

# STUDY GUIDE

The purpose of the study questions is to stimulate thought about the issues addressed in the book. This guide can be used by individuals as a way of clarifying and reflecting on the issues, but it can also be of great value to church and other ecumenical groups by using it as the basis for dialogue. By working through it in this way, participants can come face-to-face with each other's experiential truth. It can be a rich time of sharing as ideas are put forth. When in a group setting, however, intentionality must be present, to safeguard the following principles:

- Respect for every speaker and the views exchanged
- Confidentiality for any sensitive information about personal experience
- Awareness that seeking truth is a process of discernment, not a recital of absolutes
- Possibility of change in ourselves and others through dialogue

It would be best to have a trained moderator to facilitate the group process, to establish the dialogue principles and to maintain order in the group. Questions could be used in small groups or as a preparatory task for individuals coming to a large group. Stories could be role-played by individuals, or read aloud as a case study, with study questions used afterward.

It is also recommended that outside resources be used to enhance the discussion. For example, PFLAG (Parents and Friends of Lesbians and Gays) local chapters have persons who are willing to bring their personal experience to share. They can often identify a gay, lesbian, bisexual, or transgendered person who is able to speak from personal experience to the group.

Finally, a Bible study based on the parable of the great banquet (Luke 14:16–24 and Matthew 22:1–10) could help to understand the concepts at the end of Chapter 10.

## HELP FOUND IN THE
## APPENDIX BIBLIOGRAPHIES

To understand more about:

- the coming out process, see especially Borhek, Fairchild, and Switzer in the Pastoral Issues section

- same sex relationships, see especially Berzon and McDonald, in the Pastoral Issues section

- sexuality and spirituality, see especially Kelsey, Nelson, and Mollenkott in the Revising a Christian Moral Code section

- a Christian moral code for all orientations, see Cahill, Gudorf, Kosnik, and Wood in the Revising a Christian Moral Code section

- bisexuality and transgender issues, see especially Bullough, Hill, Hutchins, Klein, and Wishik in the Other Contextual Books section

- the Church's response, see especially Alexander and Preston, and Hilton in the Theology and Homosexuality section

## STUDY QUESTIONS

### *CHAPTER 1*

1. How were differences such as race, culture, beliefs, and values noted and handled in your family or community of origin? What are your memories about this that are especially vivid?

2. When did you first become aware that not everyone is heterosexual? How did this awareness make you feel?

3. Recall the time when you first knowingly met a person whose sexual orientation was not heterosexual. Describe the scene and describe the emotions you had. What happened next?

4. How and why do generalizations and stereotypes about people develop?

5. What are ways that we can resist generalizing or stereotyping non-heterosexuals in order to be more loving and just? What stands in the way of this process?

6. How do you respond to the thought that sincere Christian people can disagree on the scriptures often used to condemn homosexuality? How do you relate to those with whom you may disagree?

7. Was there ever a time when you experienced a difference between what the Church is teaching and what you feel Jesus was teaching? How did you resolve this?

## CHAPTER 2

1. How many gay, lesbian, bisexual, or transgendered people do you know personally?

2. Imagine that there is someone like Larry in your congregation. How would he be treated by you? by other worshipers? by the clergy?

3. How do you feel about Larry's parents and the teaching they received in their church while Larry was growing up? What does your church teach?

4. How could Larry have married and had children if he was supposedly gay? What was the moral choice for him in deciding whether or not to marry? in deciding whether or not to divorce?

5. What role do you feel the Church should play in ministering to people such as Larry?

## CHAPTER 3

1. Have you ever seen a Pride Parade in the media or on television? What do you think of such events?

2. What types of persons would participate in a Pride event?

3. What are some of the risks for the various persons seen taking part in a Pride activity?

4. Are there any churches in your region that have ministries to gay, lesbian, bisexual, and transgendered persons? Describe those ministries and their purpose.

5. Why would some gay, lesbian, bisexual, and transgendered persons hate the Church and/or God?

## CHAPTER 5

1. How did Nicholas first respond to the thought that he might be gay? What led him to think he might be gay?

2. Where can people who are struggling with sexual identity go to safely talk or learn more about it?

3. What are some reasons why persons struggling with sexual identity may keep this problem from their parents?

4. What part did Nicholas think his pastor would play in his "coming out" process? Was this a reasonable expectation?

5. How do you feel about Nicholas's pastor bringing five church men to his home to confront Nicholas about his homosexuality? Would something like this happen in your church? Why or why not?

6. If a person who has grown up in the Church discovers that he or she is gay, what is the best thing for that person to do in relation to the pastor and parishioners?

7. How could knowing such persons since their childhood as part of church life affect the pastor and congregation's attitude toward them?

8. What is your denomination's policy on the ordination of homosexuals? Do you agree with it? Why or why not?

9. What sort of direction should a pastor give to a non-heterosexual person who is feeling called to ordained ministry?

10. What were the considerations for Rich as he thought about serving his own denomination, which does not ordain self-avowed, practicing homosexuals, another denomination that does ordain them, or a predominately non-heterosexual denomination?

## CHAPTER 6

1. If one of your family members were to "come out," which person or persons would be most open to talking about it? Which one(s) would be most closed?

2. If you were the brother in the story of Karen, would you rather that she had "come out" during her life, or that she would keep her alienating secret until death? Why?

3. Why do you think it was helpful for the support group to meet with family members after Karen's death from the perspective of the brother and sister-in-law from the perspective of the group?

4. In the story of Bob, why was Bob both frightened and elated when he found himself so attracted to Ken in the bookstore?

5. In what ways was Bob's experience of falling in love similar to that of a woman and a man falling in love? How do you feel about this comparison?

6. Are there places in your community where non-heterosexuals can go to socialize safely? If so, do people know where such places are? If not, where would you say non-heterosexuals go for social outlets?

7. How do you feel about the scene where Ken was beaten to death? Why do you think no arrests were made in the case?

8. In the story of Charlene, why do you think she got married so many times? How do you feel about this?

9. Would you have the same feelings about Charlene's situation if she had not had any children while married?

10. Have you ever known someone who discovered he or she was gay while in a heterosexual marriage? What happened? What should the role of the Church be in such situations?

## CHAPTER 7

1. Have you or someone you know ever been to a holy union ceremony? What do you think of the idea?

2. Had you thought that the problems in planning such a ceremony might be equal to or greater than the ones faced by heterosexual couples? Why or why not?

3. What pastoral function do holy unions have for couples who cannot be legally married?

4. What should the role of the Church be regarding loving, committed, non-heterosexual relationships?

5. How do you feel about non-heterosexual couples raising children together? Why do you feel the way you do?

6. Regarding the story of Stewart and Tim, how do you feel about their use of the terms "Daddy" and "Papa"?

7. If you, like Russell, in the story of Russell and Carl, were forced to hide almost everything about your personal relationship at your workplace, where would you get your emotional and social support?

8. What would have been the most difficult aspects of Carl's hospital stay for Russell? for Carl? for Carl's family?

9. Why do you suppose Russell would work in a place where he had to be so secretive about Carl?

10. What should the role of the Church be in situations where someone's non-heterosexual partner is seriously ill or dies?

11. Which of the twelve personal stories touched you the most. Why?

## CHAPTER 8

1. How do you respond to the concept of a broad spectrum of sexual orientations that includes bisexual and transgendered individuals?

2. Why do you think bisexuals are misunderstood and even mistrusted by many homosexuals and heterosexuals alike?

3. What kind of direction do you think a bisexual person would be seeking from the Church?

4. Why do you think Betty would come to a social gathering where her unusual appearance may create some discomfort among other guests?

5. How would you have responded to Betty?

6. How do you feel about people like Betty? Why?

7. Would Betty be welcome in your church?

8. In the story of Dawn, how would you have responded to her if you were a nurse or doctor? a chaplain?

9. How do you feel about people who are not comfortable with their gender?

10. What is the role of the Church in relating to transgendered persons?

## CHAPTER 9

1. How do you use scripture, tradition, reason, and experience in discussions about sexual orientation?

2. Why do you think the author presents the life experience of gay, lesbian, bisexual, and transgendered persons as truth equal to the importance of scripture, tradition, and reason?

3. How is the Holy Spirit at work in the process of discerning truth in this or any other area of life?

## CHAPTER 10

1. How many non-heterosexual persons would you guess are present in your congregation?

2. If you are not aware of any, are there attitudes in your congregation that would discourage a gay, lesbian, bisexual, or transgendered person from being open? What are those attitudes?

3. How are attitudes toward non-heterosexual persons conveyed in your parish?

4.  Has anyone in your church come out as a gay, lesbian, bisexual, or transgendered person or as the family member of such a person? What was your response? The response of other churchgoers?

5.  How do you feel about knowing there are special places of worship primarily for non-heterosexual persons? Why do you feel this way?

6.  How do you feel about the fact that there are support groups in many colleges for gay, lesbian, bisexual, and transgendered students, faculty, and staff persons? Why do you feel this way?

7.  In what ways is the need for community among non-heterosexual persons valid or invalid, in your opinion?

8.  What, in your view, are the most obvious reasons the Church has been unable to respond to the special needs of gay, lesbian, bisexual, and transgendered persons?

9.  What do you think is meant by the terms "homosexual lifestyle" and "homosexual agenda"? Are these fair terms? Why or why not?

10. How do you respond to myths about gay, lesbian, bisexual, and transgendered persons, for example, that they are all promiscuous, child molesters, or trying to convert straight people to becoming gay?

11. What role has the media played in perpetuating stereotypes of gay, lesbian, bisexual, and transgendered persons?

12. How has sexism contributed to attitudes toward non-heterosexual persons?

13. How can the Church help us to overcome fears of persons who have sexual orientations different from our own?

14. What is the parallel between the Parable of the Great Banquet in Luke 14 and Matthew 22 and the author's view that Jesus would have us include and affirm all sexual orientations?

### CHAPTERS 11 through 15

1.  How do you understand the difference between the sin model, illness model, and variance model of attitudes toward non-heterosexual persons? Which model is operative for you? For your congregation?

2.  Why would the author feel that it is both bad and good to have a specifically gay newspaper?

3. What are some positive ways of using the media to help greater society understand sexual orientation issues?

4. Which biblical passages do you think help most to spell out a sexual moral code for Christians?

5. Why does the author say that our current Christian sexual moral code is inadequate for all sexual orientations? Do you agree? Why or why not?

6. Where do you think gay, lesbian, bisexual, and transgendered persons are getting moral guidelines, if not from the Church?

7. Do you share the author's view that, because the Church's historic misinterpretation of Scripture has caused fear and injustice toward non-heterosexual persons, the Church has a unique responsibility to society to correct this? Why or why not?

8. What point is the author trying to make about embracing all sexual orientations by citing baptism as the foundation for all Christians' call to ministry?

9. How is your vision for the Church regarding inclusion of non-heterosexual persons similar to or different from the author's?

10. Why will it take time for the Church to build trust among gay, lesbian, bisexual and transgendered persons?

11. How do you define heresy? Do you believe that an alternate voice about sexual orientation such as the author's is really heresy?

12. What do you see as signs of hope for a church more inclusive of all sexual orientations? How can you help as an individual? as a congregation? as a denomination?

# APPENDIX

## Biblical Passages on Homosexuality

The following seven biblical passages are frequently used in discussions of homosexuality:

- Genesis 19:1–29
- Leviticus 18:22
- Leviticus 20:13
- Judges 19:1–30
- Romans 1:26–27
- 1 Corinthians 6:9–11
- 1 Timothy 1:10

## Books on Theology and Homosexuality

Alexander, Marilyn Bennett, and Preston, James. *We Were Baptized Too: Claiming God's Grace for Lesbians and Gays*. Louisville, Kentucky: Westminster John Knox Press, 1996.

Boswell, John. *Christianity, Social Tolerance and Homosexuality: Gay People in Western Europe from the Beginning of the Christian Era to the Fourteenth Century*. Chicago: University of Chicago Press, 1980.

Brown, Robert McAfee. *Theology in a New Key*. Philadelphia: Westminster Press, 1981.

Cobb, John B., Jr. *Matters of Life and Death*. Louisville, Kentucky: Westminster/John Knox Press, 1991.

Edwards, George R. *Gay/Lesbian Liberation: A Biblical Perspective.* New York: Pilgrim Press, 1984.

Furnish, Victor Paul. *The Moral Teaching of Paul: Selected Issues*. Nashville: Abingdon Press, 1979; revised 1985.

Geis, Sally B., and Messer, Donald E. *Caught in the Crossfire: Helping Christians Debate Homosexuality.* Nashville: Abingdon Press, 1994.

Grace, James, ed. *God, Sex, and the Social Project: The Glassboro Papers on Religion and Human Sexuality.* Lewiston, New York: Edwin Mellen Press, 1978.

Hasbany, Richard, ed. *Homosexuality and Religion.* New York: Haworth Press, 1990.

Helminiak, Daniel A. *What the Bible Really Says About Homosexuality.* Alamo Square Press, 1984.

Hiltner, Seward. *Sex and the Christian Life.* New York: Association Press, 1957.

Hilton, Bruce. *Can Homophobia Be Cured? Wrestling with the Questions that Challenge the Church.* Nashville: Abingdon Press, 1992.

McNeill, John J. *The Church and the Homosexual.* Boston: Beacon Press, 1976; revised 1985 and 1988.

Nelson, James B. *Between Two Gardens: Reflections on Sexuality and Religious Experience.* New York: Pilgrim Press, 1983.

Nelson, James B. *Embodiment: An Approach to Sexuality and Christian Theology.* Philadelphia: Fortress Press, 1979.

Scanzoni, Letha, and Mollenkott, Virginia Ramey. *Is the Homosexual My Neighbor: A Positive Christian Response: Revised and Updated.* San Francisco: Harper San Francisco, 1994.

Scroggs, Robin. *The New Testament and Homosexuality.* Philadelphia: Fortress Press, 1983.

Siker, Jeffrey S., ed. *Homosexuality in the Church: Both Sides of the Debate.* Louisville: Kentucky: Westminster/John Knox Press, 1994.

Spong, John S. *Living in Sin? A Bishop Rethinks Human Sexuality.* San Francisco: Harper San Francisco, 1990.

White, Mel. *Stranger at the Gate: To Be Gay and Christian in America.* New York: Penguin, 1994.

## Books on Pastoral Issues

Berzon, Betty. *Permanent Partners: Building Gay and Lesbian Relationships That Last.* New York: Dutton/Plume, 1988.

Bess, Howard H. *Pastor, I Am Gay.* Palmer, Alaska: Palmer Publishing Company, 1995.

Borhek, Mary V. *Coming Out to Parents: A Two-Way Survival Guide for Lesbians and Gay Men and Their Parents.* New York: Pilgrim Press, 1983; revised 1993.

Coffin, William Sloane. *The Courage to Love.* San Francisco: Harper San Francisco, 1982.

Fairchild, Betty. *Now That You Know: What Every Parent Should Know About Homosexuality.* New York: Harcourt Brace Jovanovich, 1979; revised 1989.

Fortunato, John E. *Embracing the Exile: Healing Journeys to Gay Christians.* San Francisco: Harper San Francisco, 1985.

Glaser, Chris. *Come Home! Reclaiming Spirituality and Community as Gay Men and Lesbians.* San Francisco: Harper San Francisco, 1990.

MacPike, Laralee, ed. *There's Something I've Been Meaning to Tell You: An Anthology About Lesbian and Gay Men Coming Out to Their Children.* Tallahassee, Florida: Naiad Press, 1989.

Marcus, Eric. *Is it a Choice?* San Francisco: Harper San Francisco, 1993.

McDonald, Helen B., and Steinhorn, Audrey I. *Understanding Homosexuality: A Guide for Those Who Know, Love or Counsel Gay and Lesbian Individuals.* New York: Crossroad Books, 1993.

McNaught, Brian. *On Being Gay: Thoughts on Family, Faith and Love.* New York: St. Martin's Press, 1988.

Rench, Janice E. *Understanding Sexual Identity: A Book for Gay Teens and Their Friends.* Minneapolis: Lerner Publication, 1990.

Singer, Bennett L., ed. *Growing Up Gay: A Literary Anthology.* New York: The New Press, 1993.

Switzer, David K., and Switzer, Shirley A. *Parents of the Homosexual.* Philadelphia: Westminster Press, 1980.

## Books on Revising A Christian Moral Code

Cahill, Lisa. *Between the Sexes: Foundation for a Christian Ethics of Sexuality.* Philadelphia: Fortress Press, 1985.

Donnelly, Dody. *Radical Love: An Approach to Sexual Spirituality.* Minneapolis: Winston Press, 1984.

Gudorf, Christine E. *Body, Sex, and Pleasure: Reconstructing Christian Sexual Ethics.* Cleveland: Pilgrim Press, 1994.

Hiltner, Seward. *Sex Ethics and the Kinsey Reports.* New York: Association Press, 1953.

Kelsey, Morton and Barbara. *Sacrament of Sexuality: The Spirituality and Psychology of Sex.* Warwick, New York: Amity, 1986.

Kosnik, Anthony, ed. *Human Sexuality: New Directions in American Catholic Thought.* New York: Paulist Press, 1977.

Mollenkott, Virginia Ramey. *Sensuous Spirituality.* New York: Crossroad, 1993.

Pittenger, Norman. *Time for Consent: A Christian's Approach to Homosexuality.* London: SCM Press, 1976.

Thielicke, Helmut. *The Ethics of Sex.* New York: Harper & Row, 1964.

Wood, Frederic C., Jr. *Sex and the New Morality.* New York: Association Press, 1968.

## Other Books

Bailey, Derrick S. *Homosexuality and the Western Tradition.* London: Longmans, Grenn and Co., 1955.

Bell, Alan P., and Weinberg, Martin S. *Homosexualities: A Study of Diversity Among Men and Women.* New York: Simon & Schuster, 1978.

Bell, Alan P., and Weinberg, Martin S. *Homosexualities and Sexual Preference: Development in Men and Women.* New York: Simon & Schuster, 1981.

Boston Lesbian Psychologies Collective, ed. *Lesbian Psychologies: Explorations and Challenges.* Champaign, Illinois: University of Illinois Press, 1987.

Bullough, Vern L., and Bullough, Bonnie. *Cross Dressing, Sex and Gender.* Philadelphia: University of Pennsylvania Press, 1993.

Gonsiorek, John C., ed. *Homosexuality and Psychotherapy: A Practitioner's Handbook of Affirmative Models.* New York: Harrington Park Press, 1982.

Hart, John, and Richardson, Diane. *The Theory and Practice of Homosexuality.* London: Routledge and Kegan Paul, 1981.

Hill, Ivan, ed. *The Bisexual Spouse: Different Dimensions in Human Sexuality.* Barlina Books, 1987.

Hutchins, Loraine, and Lani Kaahumanu, ed. *BI Any Other Name: Bisexual People Speak Out.* Boston: Alyson, 1991.

Klein, Fritz. *The Bisexual Option.* New York: Harrington Park Press, 1993.

Koertge, Noretta, ed. *The Nature and Causes of Homosexuality: A Philosophic and Scientific Inquiry.* New York: Haworth Press, 1981.

Lewes, Kenneth. *The Psychoanalytic Theory of Homosexuality.* New York: Simon & Schuster, 1988.

Moses, A. Elfin, and Hawkins, Robert O. *Counseling Lesbian Women and Gay Men: A Life-Issues Approach.* Englewood Cliffs, N.J.: Prentice Hall, 1982.

Paul, Williams, and Weinrich, James D., eds. *Homosexuality: Social, Psychological and Biological Issues.* Thousand Oaks, California: Sage Publications, 1982.

Schoenberg, Robert, and Goldberg, Richard, ed. *Homosexuality and Social Work.* New York: Haworth Press, 1984.

The United Church of Christ. *Human Sexuality: A Preliminary Study.* New York: United Church Press, 1977.

Wishik, Heather, and Pierce, Carol. *Sexual Orientation and Identity: Heterosexual, Lesbian, Gay and Bisexual Journeys.* New Dynamics Publications, 1995.

Woodman, Natalie, Jr., and Lenna, Harry R. *Counseling with Gay Men and Women: A Guide for Facilitating Positive Life-Styles.* San Francisco: Jossey-Bass Publishers, 1980.